A GUIDE TO

CYMBELINE

The Shakespeare Handbooks

Guides available now:

- Antony and Cleopatra
- As You Like It
- The Comedy of Errors
- Cymbeline
- Hamlet
- Henry IV, Part 1
- Julius Caesar
- King Lear
- Macbeth
- Measure for Measure
- The Merchant of Venice
- The Merry Wives of Windsor
- A Midsummer Night's Dream
- Much Ado About Nothing
- Othello
- Richard II
- Romeo and Juliet
- The Tempest
- Twelfth Night
- The Winter's Tale

Further titles in preparation.

The Shakespeare Handbooks

A Guide to Cymbeline

by Alistair McCallum

Upstart Crow Publications

First published in 2021 by
Upstart Crow Publications

A CIP catalogue record for this book
is available from the British Library

ISBN 978 1 899747 20 7

www.shakespeare-handbooks.com

Setting the scene

Shakespeare probably wrote *Cymbeline* during the period 1609–10. He was in his mid forties, and had been one of England's foremost dramatists for the past twenty years. He was a member and shareholder of the King's Men, the country's most prestigious theatre company. The company's chief patron was King James I, a great lover of the theatre, and they gave frequent performances at court.

At this stage in his life, Shakespeare seems to have taken a decisive step away from the traditional forms of comedy, tragedy and history. The plays he produced during this period – particularly *Cymbeline, The Winter's Tale* and *The Tempest* – are more enigmatic, experimental and mystical than his earlier works. Various theories have been proposed to explain this change in direction: perhaps Shakespeare was spending less time in London, and living a more contemplative life in the calmer surroundings of his home in Stratford-upon-Avon; perhaps he had grown weary of theatrical conventions; or perhaps he was simply following the changing tastes of the time. There was a practical consideration too: as well as the large open-air Globe Theatre, the company's home since the start of the century, the King's Men had recently started performing in the Blackfriars Theatre, a smaller indoor space with an intimate, candlelit atmosphere. This venue offered exciting new possibilities in terms of sound, lighting, and special effects, all of which Shakespeare was quick to exploit in these later works.

Cymbeline is generally considered the strangest of Shakespeare's plays. The setting is a mixture of ancient and modern; the plot combines history, myth, and folk tale; and events are driven on by coincidence and confusion as much as by human intention. Critics have struggled to classify *Cymbeline*. Is it a comedy? A tragicomedy? A romance? Regardless of definitions, this strange, eventful tale of loss and deception, of reunion and redemption, provides an exhilarating and uplifting experience for audiences:

"Critics have difficulty with Cymbeline. *Theatregoers feel otherwise. Problems of genre, and even of inconsistent characterization, disappear in the delight of enthralling spectacle, a succession of splendid surprises, and constant theatrical suspense: three hours of wonder. In performance, the play appears the work of a superb dramatic craftsman at the very height of his virtuosity."*

Levi Fox, *The Shakespeare Handbook*, 1987

A state of disharmony

The ever-expanding Roman Empire, led by Augustus Caesar, is threatening the shores of Britain. Fifty years ago, Augustus' predecessor, Julius Caesar, had staged an invasion of the kingdom; and the invading army only withdrew when the Britons agreed to pay an annual levy to the empire in return for the kingdom's peace and safety.

In recent years, the British king Cymbeline has neglected to make these payments, confident that Britain can successfully resist another invasion. However, it is impossible that Augustus Caesar will ignore Britain's provocation, and the prospect of war cannot be taken lightly.

The troublesome relationship with Rome is not Cymbeline's only concern. He has family problems, too: his daughter, the princess Imogen, has married without his permission, refusing even to contemplate the husband chosen for her by Cymbeline and his wife.

Unable to see a way out of his present difficulties, the king is in a constant state of anxiety. A mood of pessimism hangs over the royal court like a dark cloud, and the king's courtiers can only look on helplessly.

Curtain up

A troubled king

Two gentlemen at the court of Cymbeline, King of Britain, are discussing the latest news. There is a gloomy atmosphere at court; but one of the men, a court insider, suggests that the general unhappiness may be apparent rather than real. Courtiers are notorious, he points out, for their insincerity. With their show of anxiety, perhaps they are simply imitating the king:

1st Gentleman: You do not meet a man but frowns.[1] Our bloods
No more obey the heavens than our courtiers
Still seem as does the king.[2]

[1] *who does not frown*
[2] *in the same way as our characters are dictated by the heavens, courtiers always mimic the king's outward behaviour*

The reason for the king's displeasure, it now emerges, is the recent marriage of his daughter Imogen.

The king's first wife, mother of princess Imogen, died some time ago, and he has now remarried. His second wife is herself a widow, with a son named Cloten; and both the king and his new queen were keen to see the marriage of Imogen to Cloten. Imogen, however, has dashed their hopes by marrying another man, Posthumus Leonatus, without their consent. The king, furious at his daughter's disobedience, has imprisoned Imogen at court and ordered Posthumus to leave the kingdom.

The distress felt by Cymbeline, however, is not shared by his followers despite their apparent sadness:

1st Gentleman: … not a courtier,
Although they wear their faces to the bent
Of the king's looks,[1] hath a heart that is not
Glad at the thing they scowl at.

[1] *although they all put on expressions that match the king's dejected appearance*

Cloten is universally despised, the gentleman reveals, and there is a general sense of relief that the princess has avoided the fate of marrying him. Posthumus, on the other hand, is widely regarded as virtuous and honourable, a worthy husband for the woman who is next in line to the throne of Britain.

Posthumus, the gentleman goes on to explain, was an orphan. His father Leonatus had been a renowned warrior in Britain's struggle against the invading Roman Empire. Having lost two sons in the wars, Leonatus eventually died of grief; and his wife too died as she was giving birth to their third son.

This child, given the name Posthumus, was brought up in Cymbeline's court. The boy was bright and good-natured, and gained the admiration of the whole court as he grew to adulthood. Posthumus' worth is confirmed, the gentleman declares, by the fact that princess Imogen has fallen in love with him and married him.

Imogen, it appears, is the king's only child. However, the gentleman now reveals a strange and disturbing event in Cymbeline's past:

1st Gentleman: He had two sons – if this be worth your hearing,
Mark it[1] – the eldest of them at three years old,
I'th' swathing clothes[2] the other, from their nursery
Were stolen, and to this hour no guess in knowledge[3]
Which way they went.

[1] *take notice of it, don't forget it*
[2] *in swaddling clothes; still a baby*
[3] *there have been no informed guesses; no one has a clear idea*

The abduction of the two children happened about twenty years ago. It seems incredible, the gentleman's companion remarks, that a king's sons could have disappeared in this way:

2nd Gentleman: That a king's children should be so conveyed,[1]
So slackly guarded, and the search so slow
That could not trace them!
1st Gentleman: Howsoe'er 'tis strange,[2]
Or that the negligence may well be laughed at,
Yet is it true, sir.

[1] *stolen away*
[2] *however strange it may be*

A cruel separation

The two gentlemen hurry away as the queen approaches. She is in conversation with the young couple, Imogen and Posthumus.

The queen assures Imogen that she will not play the role of the wicked stepmother, so often portrayed in folk tales. In fact, she will work to release her stepdaughter from the captivity ordered by the king:

Queen: No, be assured you shall not find me, daughter,
After the slander[1] of most stepmothers,
Evil-eyed unto you. You're my prisoner, but
Your jailer shall deliver you the keys
That lock up your restraint.

[1] *as in the conventional, unjust image*

The queen turns to Posthumus, who is shortly to be banished, and promises that she will do her best to help him too. However, the king is still in an angry frame of mind, she warns, and for the time being Posthumus should accept the sentence handed down to him.

As a favour to the young couple, the queen leaves them on their own to say a final farewell before Posthumus leaves the country. She realises that, in doing so, she is going against Cymbeline's command:

Queen: I'll fetch a turn[1] about the garden, pitying
The pangs of barred affections,[2] though the king
Hath charged[3] you should not speak together.

[1] *take a walk*
[2] *the pain of your forbidden love*
[3] *ordered*

As soon as the queen is out of earshot, Imogen makes it clear that she does not trust her stepmother in the slightest:

Imogen: O dissembling[1] courtesy! How fine this tyrant
Can tickle[2] where she wounds!

[1] *deceitful*
[2] *flatter, charm*

Imogen weeps as she foresees a lonely life in the hostile surroundings of her father's court, comforted only by the hope that one day she may be reunited with her husband. Posthumus, vowing to be faithful to Imogen even in exile, is on the verge of tears too. Banished from Britain, he will live in Rome with Philario, a friend of his late father's. Knowing that he will be desperate to hear from Imogen, he urges her to write often:

Posthumus: … thither[1] write, my queen,[2]
And with mine eyes I'll drink the words you send,
Though ink be made of gall.[3]

[1] *there; to Philario's house in Rome*
[2] *mistress; ruler of my heart*
[3] *even if the ink were bitter and noxious*

The queen returns briefly to hurry the couple along; she is worried, she tells them, that the king may pass by at any minute and scold her for allowing them to meet. As she slips away, however, she secretly reveals that she will ensure that the king does see them together. Even when she offends the king, she always manages to benefit from the situation:

Queen: [*aside*] Yet I'll move him
To walk this way.[1] I never do him wrong
But he does buy my injuries to be friends,
Pays dear for my offences.[2]

[1] *I'll make sure that he comes in this direction, so that he can see Posthumus and Imogen together*
[2] *even when I cause him offence, he treats me as if I were doing him a favour, and ends up indebted to me for my wrongdoing*

Posthumus and Imogen, knowing that they will very soon be parted, exchange tokens of their love. Imogen gives her husband a precious ring that belonged to her mother, now dead; but in her despair she suggests that one day he may no longer wish to keep it. That day will never come, Posthumus vows:

Imogen: … This diamond was my mother's. Take it, heart,
[*gives him a ring*]
But[1] keep it till you woo another wife,
When Imogen is dead.
Posthumus: How, how? Another?
You gentle gods, give me but this I have[2] …

[1] *only*
[2] *just allow me to be with my one true wife*

In return, Posthumus places a bracelet on his wife's arm. His gift is less valuable, he confesses. He has gained in the exchange just as he did when, as a penniless orphan, he won the love of a princess:

Posthumus: … As I my poor self did exchange for you
To your so infinite loss, so in our trifles
I still win of you.[1] For my sake wear this:
[*puts a bracelet on her arm*]

It is a manacle of love. I'll place it
Upon this fairest prisoner.

[1] *in our exchange of tokens I gain more than you do, just as I did when we fell in love*

Banishment

The couple's loving, sorrowful farewell is suddenly interrupted by the arrival of Cymbeline and his entourage. When the king catches sight of Posthumus, he cannot contain his anger; the young man has been sentenced to banishment, and should have left the country by now. He orders him to depart immediately, on pain of death. Posthumus, remaining calm and courteous, takes his leave:

Cymbeline: Thou basest thing, avoid hence,[1] from my sight!
If after this command thou fraught the court
With thy unworthiness,[2] thou diest. Away!
Thou'rt poison to my blood.
Posthumus: The gods protect you
And bless the good remainders of the court.[3]
I am gone.

[1] *get away from this place*
[2] *you inflict your disreputable presence on the court*
[3] *the good people remaining at court*

Imogen cries out desperately as her husband leaves. Cymbeline turns on her furiously, accusing her of tormenting him in his old age. She has shown deliberate disobedience by marrying a commoner, a man of no social standing, rather than the husband chosen for her. She is next in line to the throne, and her marriage is a matter of great importance. Imogen, in response, argues that Posthumus is an admirable addition to the royal family:

Cymbeline: Thou took'st a beggar, wouldst have made my throne
A seat for baseness.[1]
Imogen: No, I rather added
A lustre[2] to it.

[1] *a source of shame and dishonour*
[2] *brilliance*

Impervious to her father's criticism, Imogen reminds him that he was the one who rescued Posthumus as a young orphan, nurturing him at court almost as if the boy were his own son. She wishes, in her distress, that she were the daughter of a shepherd, not a king, and that Posthumus too was no more than a local herdsman's son.

The queen now approaches, and for a moment Cymbeline directs his anger at her: by allowing the couple to meet before their separation, she has disobeyed his instructions. His attention quickly returns to his daughter, however, and he orders his attendants to confine her to her room. The queen, with a show of sympathy towards Imogen, persuades Cymbeline to relent. Still complaining bitterly, he leaves the two women together:

Queen: Sweet sovereign,
Leave us to ourselves, and make yourself some comfort
Out of your best advice.[1]
Cymbeline: Nay, let her languish
A drop of blood a day[2] and, being aged,
Die of this folly. [*leaves with his lords*]

[1] *spend some time in calm reflection, and you will feel less troubled*
[2] *grow weak as her grief gradually eats up her vitality*

The queen and Imogen are now joined by Pisanio, Posthumus' servant. Pisanio reports that the queen's son Cloten drew his sword and attempted to attack Posthumus as he left the court. The servant hints that Posthumus is far superior to Cloten as a swordsman, and dealt with his attacker calmly and safely:

Pisanio: My lord your son[1] drew on my master.
Queen: Ha?
No harm, I trust, is done?
Pisanio: There might have been,
But that my master rather played than fought
And had no help of anger.[2]

[1] *Cloten*
[2] *was not motivated by anger; maintained his self-control*

Imogen asks Pisanio why he has left his master rather than accompanying him to the port, where his ship is waiting to take him into exile. Pisanio replies that Posthumus has instructed him to return to court and become Imogen's servant. Desperate for news of any kind about her husband, Imogen asks him to follow him again to the port; when the ship has left, Pisanio is to return and tell her everything about his departure.

Self-delusion

I, ii

After his unsuccessful attack on Posthumus, Cloten is sweating profusely, and one of his attendants advises him to change his clothes. Cloten asks, hopefully, whether he has drawn blood from his opponent. Another attendant remarks, out of his master's hearing, that Posthumus was barely inconvenienced by the encounter:

1st Lord: Sir, I would advise you to shift[1] a shirt. The violence of action hath made you reek as a sacrifice[2] …
Cloten: If my shirt were bloody, then to shift it.[3] Have I hurt him?
2nd Lord: [*aside*] No, faith, not so much as his patience.[4]

[1] *change*
[2] *like the body of a burning sacrificial animal*
[3] *if there's blood on my shirt, it would be a good idea to change it*
[4] *you have not even tried his patience*

Cloten boasts that Posthumus was afraid to fight with him, but another sarcastic comment from his attendant suggests that the opposite was the case:

Cloten: The villain would not stand me.[1]
2nd Lord: [*aside*] No, but he fled forward still,[2] toward your face.

[1] *stand his ground, face up to me*
[2] *continually*

It is clear that Cloten deeply resents the fact that Imogen has rejected him, instead choosing Posthumus as her husband. One of his companions argues, unconvincingly, that the princess is not bright enough to appreciate Cloten's good qualities. The other has a less flattering opinion, though he is careful not to let his master know:

Cloten: … that she should love this fellow and refuse me!
2nd Lord: [*aside*] If it be a sin to make a true election,[1] she is damned.
1st Lord: Sir, as I told you always, her beauty and her brain go not together. She's a good sign,[2] but I have seen small reflection of her wit.[3]

[1] *a sound choice*
[2] *she has a good outward appearance*
[3] *evidence of her intelligence*

The exile begins — I, iii

As instructed by Imogen, Pisanio has been to the port to witness Posthumus' departure. He is now back at court, and Imogen is questioning him urgently, desperate to know everything that happened as the ship set sail. Posthumus' parting words, reports Pisanio, were of his beloved wife. Imogen can hardly contain her distress:

Imogen: What was the last
That he spake to thee?
Pisanio: It was his queen, his queen.
Imogen: Then waved his handkerchief?
Pisanio: And kissed it, madam.
Imogen: Senseless[1] linen, happier therein than I!

[1] *inanimate; unfeeling*

If she had been at the port, says Imogen, she would have stayed until her husband disappeared from view completely. She imagines him vanishing as his ship sails into the distance:

Imogen: I would have broke mine eye-strings,[1] cracked them, but[2]
To look upon him till the diminution
Of space had pointed him sharp as my needle;[3]

Nay, followed him till he had melted from
The smallness of a gnat to air, and then
Have turned mine eye and wept.

[1] *tissues attached to the eye, believed to break when a person went blind or died*
[2] *just*
[3] *had made him seem as tiny as the point of a needle*

There are so many things, Imogen complains, that she wished to say to Posthumus before the king forced him to leave so abruptly. She wanted her husband to know that she intends to think about him and pray at certain times of day. Above all, she wanted him to promise that he would remain faithful:

Imogen: Ere[1] I could tell him
How I would think on him at certain hours,
Such thoughts and such,[2] or I could make him swear
The shes[3] of Italy should not betray
Mine interest[4] and his honour, or have charged him
At the sixth hour of morn, at noon, at midnight,
T'encounter me with orisons[5] …
… comes in my father,
And, like the tyrannous breathing of the north,
Shakes all our buds from growing.[6]

[1] *before*
[2] *how I would think about him in various ways at different times of day*
[3] *women*
[4] *my right to him, as his wife*
[5] *to join me in my prayers*
[6] *interrupts us, like the relentless north wind which disturbs young buds and stops them from growing*

> *"Loving and candid, resourceful, witty, and a little rash, Imogen stands at the centre of the play. The characters who surround her, although powerfully and effectively drawn, are less complex."*
>
> Anne Barton, Programme notes for the RSC production of *Cymbeline*, 1974

A difference of opinion

I, iv

In Rome, Philario is hosting a cosmopolitan gathering. Individuals from France, Spain and Holland are present, as well as his fellow Italian, the nobleman Iachimo. The men are discussing the imminent arrival of a Briton, Posthumus, who is to be a guest at Philario's house.

Even here in Italy, Posthumus is renowned for his honour and integrity. Iachimo, however, has his doubts. Perhaps the Briton's marriage to a princess has given him a higher status than he truly deserves:

Iachimo: This matter of marrying his king's daughter, wherein he must be weighed rather by her value than his own,[1] words him, I doubt not, a great deal from the matter.[2]

[1] *which enhances his reputation through his wife's worth and rank, rather than demonstrating his own intrinsic value*

[2] *encourages people to praise him in a way that he does not deserve in reality*

Posthumus' banishment has only increased his popularity, remarks Iachimo cynically, and serves as a distraction from the fact that he is socially inferior to princess Imogen. He wonders how his friend Philario came to know the Briton. Philario replies that, as a soldier, he fought side by side with Posthumus' father, Leonatus, who saved his life on many occasions. At this moment, Posthumus himself arrives, and Philario urges his guests to treat him courteously.

It immediately becomes apparent that one of Philario's friends, a Frenchman, has already met Posthumus. Although their exchanges are polite and cordial, it emerges that the occasion of their meeting was dramatic and potentially fatal. On an earlier visit to France, Posthumus had got into a quarrel which was on the verge of developing into a sword fight; Philario's friend had stepped in to break up the duel, quite possibly saving Posthumus' life.

Posthumus remembers the incident well, and is still grateful to the Frenchman for his intervention. He was young and immature at the time, explains Posthumus, and too quick to take offence over a relatively trivial matter.

Iachimo's curiosity is immediately piqued: what was the nature of this quarrel that almost led to bloodshed? It emerges that the young Posthumus had become involved in a heated dispute over the merits of British women compared with those of France. He had argued passionately in favour of the women of Britain, and his own sweetheart in particular:

Frenchman: … this gentleman[1] at that time vouching – and upon warrant of bloody affirmation[2] – his to be more fair, virtuous, wise, chaste, constant, qualified[3] and less attemptable[4] than any the rarest[5] of our ladies in France.

1 *Posthumus*
2 *ready to back up his assertion with violence if necessary*
3 *accomplished, talented*
4 *vulnerable to seduction, liable to be unfaithful*
5 *any of the most admirable*

Iachimo, who takes a more jaundiced view of women in general, dismisses the idea of the perfect, incorruptible woman; the Briton's beloved cannot be such a paragon of virtue. Posthumus springs to the defence of his wife:

Iachimo: That lady[1] is not now living, or this gentleman's opinion, by this, worn out.[2]
Posthumus: She holds her virtue still, and I my mind.[3]

1 *the lady who was the subject of the quarrel; Imogen*
2 *Posthumus must have lost his idealistic view by now*
3 *she is just as virtuous now as she was then, and my opinion has not changed*

Imogen cannot be superior to all the women in Italy, Iachimo claims. Noticing a diamond ring on Posthumus' finger, he points out that, however fine it may be, there are doubtless others in the world that are more precious, even if he has not seen them. In the same way, there must be women that Posthumus has never met who far excel Imogen.

Posthumus refuses to accept Iachimo's assertion; both his ring and his beloved are without equal in his eyes. Iachimo mocks his attachment to the ring. If it is the most valuable thing in the world, as he claims, Imogen must come a poor second. The two cannot be compared, declares Posthumus:

Iachimo: What do you esteem it at? [1]
Posthumus: More than the world enjoys. [2]
Iachimo: Either your unparagoned mistress is dead, or she's outprized by a trifle. [3]
Posthumus: You are mistaken: the one may be sold or given, or if there were wealth enough for the purchase or merit for the gift; [4] the other is not a thing for sale, and only the gift of the gods.

[1] *how much is the ring worth to you?*
[2] *more than all the world's wealth*
[3] *either your incomparable beloved must be dead, or she's worth less than a trinket*
[4] *the ring could go to anyone wealthy enough to purchase it, or worthy enough to deserve it as a gift*

Italy had a reputation in Shakespeare's day as an exotic, dangerous place, a land of treachery, courtesans and conspiracies. The notorious Machiavelli had died a century before *Cymbeline* was written, but he still loomed large in the English popular imagination:

"Shakespeare makes Iachimo a contemporary Italian; the Rome he comes from is no antique world capital of eagles and classical pillars, but lies in the hot, corrupt, Machiavellian Italy which bred, so the Elizabethan English believed, 'devils incarnate'."

John Wain, *The Living World of Shakespeare*, 1964

Neither man is prepared to back down, and beneath the refined wordplay their growing hostility is becoming clear. Iachimo, determined to provoke the newcomer, now goes even further. Just as Posthumus' ring may be stolen, he suggests, his wife too may be vulnerable. Adultery happens from time to time, and Imogen, like all women, is not immune:

Iachimo: ... strange fowl light upon neighbouring ponds.[1] Your ring may be stolen too, so your brace of unprizable estimations;[2] the one is but frail and the other casual.[3] A cunning thief or a that-way-accomplished courtier[4] would hazard the winning both of first and last.[5]

[1] *just as wildfowl may visit neighbouring ponds, a man may attempt to seduce his neighbour's wife*
[2] *your two priceless possessions, your ring and your wife, may both be stolen*
[3] *one is weak and defenceless; the other is insecure, and subject to accident or misfortune*
[4] *a courtier adept at seducing women*
[5] *might attempt to possess both your ring and your wife, even if it involved a degree of risk*

Posthumus retorts that no man in Italy could ever persuade his wife to be unfaithful. He is confident that his ring too is secure even if, he remarks casually, there is no shortage of thieves in the country. At this point the host, Philario, intervenes. The argument is getting out of hand:

Posthumus: Your Italy contains none so accomplished a courtier to convince the honour[1] of my mistress ... I do nothing doubt you have store of thieves;[2] notwithstanding, I fear not[3] my ring.

Philario: Let us leave here,[4] gentlemen.

[1] *overcome, seduce*
[2] *I have no doubt that you have plenty of thieves*
[3] *I'm not worried about*
[4] *stop now*

A question of honour

Posthumus is only too glad to bring the conversation to an end, he claims. He remarks, sarcastically, that Iachimo has been very welcoming in discussing matters so freely with him on their first meeting. Iachimo, for his part, refuses to change the subject. He himself could easily seduce Imogen, he declares, if the circumstances were right:

Iachimo: With five times so much conversation[1] I should get ground of your fair mistress, make her go back even to the yielding,[2] had I admittance and opportunity to friend.[3]

[1] *with a conversation five times as long as the one we have just had*
[2] *gain the advantage over her, as in a duel, and persuade her to surrender*
[3] *if I had the chance to meet and befriend her*

Posthumus refuses to respond. Iachimo now goes even further; he is prepared to back up his words by wagering half of everything he owns on his ability to seduce Imogen. It is Posthumus' stubborn refusal to accept that his wife could ever be unfaithful, says Iachimo, that provokes him. He does not wish to insult Imogen, as he would make the same bet involving any woman. If he wins the bet, all he wants in return is Posthumus' diamond ring:

Iachimo: I dare thereupon pawn the moiety of my estate to your ring,[1] which in my opinion o'ervalues it something.[2] But I make my wager rather against your confidence than her reputation;[3] and to bar your offence herein too,[4] I durst[5] attempt it against any lady in the world.

[1] *stake half of my wealth against your ring*
[2] *rather overestimates its value*
[3] *I am betting against your overconfidence rather than Imogen's good name*
[4] *to ensure that you are not personally offended by this wager*
[5] *would dare*

Iachimo is deceiving himself, replies Posthumus. Any attempt to make advances to Imogen would be met with a firm rejection. Such an attempt would deserve severe punishment, he remarks pointedly.

The situation has now taken a sinister turn. Philario once again tries to smooth things over, but for Iachimo there is no going back. He is prepared to stake a huge amount of money on his ability to seduce Imogen. All he requires is a letter of introduction to the British court so that he can meet the princess. Posthumus, utterly confident of his wife's loyalty, is willing to gamble the diamond ring that she gave him as a parting gift:

Iachimo: I will lay you ten thousand ducats[1] to your ring that, commend me[2] to the court where your lady is, with no more advantage than the opportunity of a second conference, and I will bring from thence that honour of hers which you imagine so reserved.[3]

Posthumus: I will wage against your gold, gold to it.[4] My ring I hold dear as my finger: 'tis part of it.

1 *bet ten thousand gold coins*
2 *if you arrange a favourable introduction*
3 *as long as I can meet her more than once, I will demonstrate that her supposed loyalty to you is imaginary*
4 *I will match your stake of gold with gold of my own*

Iachimo taunts Posthumus, claiming that he is afraid to accept the wager as he knows, deep down, that Imogen would be unfaithful. Posthumus, infuriated, announces that the bet is to go ahead. Philario is horrified, but the two men are resolute:

Posthumus: Let there be covenants drawn between's.[1] My mistress exceeds in goodness the hugeness of your unworthy thinking.[2] I dare you to this match. Here's my ring.

Philario: I will have it no lay.[3]

Iachimo: By the gods, it is one.[4]

1 *a legal agreement drawn up between us*
2 *however excessive and despicable your imagination may be, Imogen's virtue is greater*
3 *I will not allow this wager to take place*
4 *the wager is valid*

Iachimo now spells out the wager to which they have both agreed. He will visit Cymbeline's court, with a letter of introduction from Posthumus that will enable him to meet princess Imogen; and if he later returns without evidence that he has successfully seduced Imogen, his stake of ten thousand gold ducats will go to Posthumus.

Posthumus adds that there is more than money at stake; if Iachimo's bragging proves to be unfounded, he is likely to pay with his life. Undaunted, Iachimo embraces the challenge enthusiastically and shakes hands with his rival. He intends to set out for Britain before either of them has a chance to reconsider:

Posthumus: … if you make your voyage upon her and give me directly to understand you have prevailed,[1] I am no further your enemy; she is not worth our debate. If she remain unseduced, you not making it appear otherwise,[2] for your ill opinion and th'assault you have made to her chastity, you shall answer me with your sword.[3]

Iachimo: Your hand, a covenant.[4] We will have these things set down by lawful counsel, and straight away for Britain, lest the bargain should catch cold and starve.[5]

[1] *if you prove to me that you have succeeded in your quest to seduce Imogen*
[2] *and you cannot give any evidence of your success*
[3] *you will have to face me in a duel*
[4] *we are agreed*
[5] *I will depart immediately, in case we cool down and call off our wager*

"Iachimo is wicked for the pure pleasure of it, for the sake of the sport. At the bottom of the business is his vanity; no woman, he is confident, can resist him ... He has a quick and sensitive mind. He can size up another man's weaknesses, and play on them with artistic skill. Posthumus proves fairly easy quarry."

Harley Granville-Barker, *Prefaces to Shakespeare*, 1930

A sinister request

Back in Cymbeline's court, the queen has arranged a visit from Cornelius, the court physician. She wishes to meet him alone, so she sends her ladies-in-waiting out to the garden to gather flowers for her room.

When Cornelius arrives, it is clear that he is worried. He has brought some drugs requested by the queen, but he feels obliged to let her know that the substances she has asked for are extremely dangerous:

Cornelius: … I beseech your grace, without offence –
My conscience bids me ask – wherefore you have
Commanded of me[1] these most poisonous compounds,
Which are the movers of a languishing death,[2]
But though slow, deadly.

[1] *why you have requested from me*
[2] *which will cause a long-drawn-out death*

Taking the box containing the drugs, the queen rebukes the doctor. She is surprised that he should ask such a question; he must be aware that she has an interest in herbs and flowers, as he has helped her to create her own perfumes. She has an enquiring mind, and wishes to extend her knowledge by experimenting with toxic compounds and their antidotes. Only a few small, insignificant creatures will suffer:

Queen: I will try the forces[1]
Of these thy compounds on such creatures as
We count not worth the hanging – but none human –
To try the vigour of them and apply
Allayments to their act,[2] and by them gather
Their several virtues and effects.[3]

[1] *examine the effects*
[2] *test the drugs' potency, and administer antidotes*
[3] *establish the properties and actions of the various compounds*

The doctor warns the queen that observing the effects of these drugs will be unpleasant and disturbing. She will need to develop a hard heart if she is to experiment in this way, he tells her, but she brushes aside his concerns.

The queen has also asked Pisanio to see her, and he now arrives. Although she maintains a friendly manner, it is clear that she does not trust the man; he was servant to Posthumus before his banishment, and is now in Imogen's service. He is undoubtedly hostile to her son Cloten, and she intends to deal with him. She wishes to speak to him in private, and asks Cornelius to leave.

As the doctor departs, he remarks secretly that the drugs he has given her are not those she requested. He realises that the queen is a dangerous individual, not to be trusted with deadly poisons. He has given her instead a mixture that will bring about a deep sleep, virtually indistinguishable from death. Anyone who takes it will not be in danger, however, and will eventually awake feeling invigorated:

Cornelius: I do know her spirit,
And will not trust one of her malice with
A drug of such damned nature. Those she has
Will stupefy and dull the sense awhile …
… but there is
No danger in what show of death it makes[1]
More than the locking up the spirits a time,
To be more fresh, reviving.[2]

[1] *in the appearance of death that the drug produces*
[2] *other than to suppress the signs of life for a while, leaving the taker refreshed on awakening*

A few years before Shakespeare wrote *Cymbeline*, his daughter Susanna had married John Hall, a physician who had recently set up a practice in Stratford-upon-Avon.

The world of medicine at the time was not generally held in high esteem; it was poorly regulated, and rife with fraudsters and charlatans. Where doctors appear in Shakespeare's early comedies, they are portrayed as incompetent figures of fun. However, Hall was a conscientious, attentive physician who gained a sound reputation in Stratford and the surrounding area. He specialised in the treatment of scurvy, a common disease at the time which was poorly understood and notoriously difficult to diagnose.

The relationship between Shakespeare and his son-in-law seems to have been one of mutual warmth and respect. Did John Hall, with his methodical approach and high ethical standards, change his father-in-law's view of the profession?

"We must always be wary of attempts to map Shakespeare's life on to his work. But writers cannot avoid drawing on their experience. Is it a coincidence that in Shakespeare's earlier works there are two comic doctors ... whereas in the plays written after John Hall's arrival in Stratford-upon-Avon, there are several dignified, sympathetically portrayed medical men? Among them are the physician who has to deal with that difficult patient Lady Macbeth, the doctor who revives the exhausted King Lear, and Dr Cornelius in Cymbeline *(who tricks the wicked stepmother, giving her a sleeping draught rather than the poison she desires)."*

Jonathan Bate, *Soul of the Age*, 2008

Ruthless ambition

Alone with Pisanio, the queen raises the subject of her stepdaughter Imogen, who is still tormented by the departure of her husband. The princess would be much happier, claims the queen, if she abandoned any idea of seeing Posthumus again; her own son Cloten would make a much more suitable husband. If Pisanio can make the princess see sense, the queen promises, he will be rewarded handsomely:

Queen: Do thou work.[1]
When thou shalt bring me word she loves my son,
I'll tell thee on the instant thou art then
As great as is thy master – greater, for
His fortunes all lie speechless, and his name
Is at last gasp.[2]

[1] *use your influence*
[2] *Posthumus' status and reputation, by now, are virtually non-existent*

While the queen is talking, she drops the box – seemingly by accident – that Cornelius has just given her. Pisanio picks it up, and the queen remarks that the contents of the box are very special. It contains a wonderfully restorative drug, she explains; and as a gesture of goodwill, she decides to allow Pisanio to keep the box. If he succeeds in winning Imogen over to the idea of marrying Cloten, the rewards will be much greater:

Queen: Thou tak'st up
Thou knowst not what;[1] but take it for thy labour.[2]
It is a thing I made which hath the king
Five times redeemed[3] from death. I do not know
What is more cordial.[4] Nay, I prithee, take it.
It is an earnest[5] of a farther good
That I mean to thee.

[1] *you don't realise what you are picking up*
[2] *as a reward for your co-operation*
[3] *rescued, saved*
[4] *I know of no other remedy that is so effective*
[5] *instalment, down payment*

The queen sends Pisanio out to summon back her ladies-in-waiting. When he has gone, it becomes clear that she is in no doubt where Pisanio's loyalties lie:

Queen: A sly and constant knave,
Not to be shaked;[1] the agent for his master[2]
And the remembrancer of her to hold
The handfast to her lord.[3]

[1] *a cunning villain whose loyalty is unshakeable*
[2] *one who will act in the interests of his master, Posthumus*
[3] *a constant reminder to Imogen to stay faithful to her marriage vows*

The queen realises that Pisanio will never attempt to change Imogen's mind as she has instructed. However, with luck he will try the medicine she gave him, believing it to be a powerful tonic; Imogen's last link with Posthumus will then be removed. And if the princess should continue to favour her husband over Cloten, she too will suffer the same fate. If her son cannot marry the princess, he must become heir to the throne himself:

Queen: I have given him that
Which, if he take, shall quite unpeople her
Of liegers for her sweet,[1] and which she after,
Except she bend her humour, shall be assured
To taste of too.[2]

[1] *will kill him, leaving no one to remind Imogen of her husband*
[2] *unless Imogen changes her attitude, she will die in the same way*

At this moment, Pisanio returns with the queen's ladies-in-waiting. The queen's manner changes in an instant as she greets them warmly. Her attendants have been picking wild flowers, and the women now leave to arrange them in the queen's private room.

With her parting words, the queen urges Pisanio to consider how much he has to gain if he sides with her and her son. When she has gone, however, Pisanio vehemently expresses his distrust of the queen and his loyalty to Posthumus:

Queen: Fare thee well, Pisanio.
Think on my words. [*she leaves*]
Pisanio: And shall do.
But when to my good lord I prove untrue,
I'll choke myself. There's all I'll do for you.

An unexpected visitor

I, vi

Imogen, alone and despondent, is contemplating her fate. Her father is cruel, and her stepmother treacherous; her beloved husband is in exile and, to make matters worse, she is being pursued by the loutish Cloten. She wishes she had not been born into the poisonous world of Cymbeline's court, but could instead live a normal, humble life. For a moment she thinks enviously of her two brothers, stolen away many years ago. If she too had been taken, she muses, she would now be happy.

Imogen's thoughts are interrupted as Pisanio enters with a visitor: it is Iachimo, who has made the journey from Rome, and he presents Imogen with letters from her beloved.

As Imogen reads, Iachimo notes her beauty with approval. However, if her virtue matches her appearance, seducing her will be no easy task. If he is to succeed, he will need to keep his nerve:

Iachimo: [*aside*] All of her that is out of door,[1] most rich.
If she be furnished with a mind so rare,[2]
She is alone th'Arabian bird,[3] and I
Have lost the wager. Boldness be my friend.

[1] *visible, external*
[2] *if her character is as exceptional as her appearance*
[3] *utterly unique and perfect; like the mythical phoenix, only one of which could exist at any time*

Delighted to hear from her husband, Imogen welcomes the newcomer warmly. However, she is mystified by his response. Rather than engaging in conversation, he starts muttering to himself anxiously. He seems to have been deeply shocked by something, and is apparently unable to contain his astonishment. Imogen, puzzled, asks what is on his mind:

Iachimo: What, are men mad? Hath nature given them eyes
To see this vaulted arch and the rich crop
Of sea and land,[1] which can distinguish 'twixt
The fiery orbs above and the twinned stones
Upon th'unnumbered beach,[2] and can we not
Partition make with spectacles so precious
'Twixt fair and foul?[3]

Imogen: What makes your admiration?[4]

[1] *the overarching sky contrasted with the earth's intricate surface of sea and land*

[2] *eyes which can tell one star from another, and even distinguish between identical pebbles on the beach*

[3] *can we not, with these miraculous organs of sight, see the difference between beauty and ugliness?*

[4] *what is causing your amazement?*

Iachimo's strange, rambling monologue continues. He makes no attempt to explain his feelings to Imogen; he seems, instead, to be thinking out loud, talking to himself rather than to her. Although his words are unclear, he appears to be wondering how a man could prefer ugliness, vice and squalor to beauty and excellence. Surely, he asks himself, the difference is clear to all, even to dumb animals?

Imogen asks the visitor again what is troubling him. Finally, without explaining exactly what his outburst meant or who he had in mind, Iachimo recovers his composure. He asks Pisanio to leave and attend to the manservant who has accompanied him from Italy. He and Imogen are now alone.

Imogen, naturally, is keen to hear first-hand news of her husband. However, the visitor's answers are unsettling. Posthumus, despite his exile and separation from his wife, is in surprisingly high spirits:

Imogen: Continues well my lord?
His health, beseech you?
Iachimo: Well, madam.
Imogen: Is he disposed to mirth? I hope he is.
Iachimo: Exceeding pleasant: none a stranger there
So merry and so gamesome.[1] He is called
The Briton Reveller.
Imogen: When he was here
He did incline to sadness,[2] and oft-times
Not knowing why.
Iachimo: I never saw him sad.

[1] *there is not another foreigner in Rome as cheerful and lively as him*
[2] *tended to be serious*

Iachimo mentions that one of Posthumus' friends in Rome, a Frenchman, has a sweetheart back at home. He misses her terribly; but Posthumus, according to Iachimo, finds it hilarious that a man should waste his time pining over an absent partner. Posthumus mocks the Frenchman mercilessly, reports Iachimo, frequently pointing out that his sweetheart is undoubtedly enjoying the company of other lovers while he is away.

Imogen is dismayed to hear of her husband's attitude. Iachimo offers his sympathy both to her and to Posthumus, making her even more distressed. Her suspicions, already aroused by the visitor's earlier outburst, are now unbearable. When Iachimo hints at the Briton's disreputable behaviour, Imogen demands a straight answer:

Iachimo: Whilst I am bound to wonder,[1] I am bound
To pity, too.
Imogen: What do you pity, sir?
Iachimo: Two creatures heartily.
Imogen: Am I one, sir?
You look on me. What wrack discern you in me[2]
Deserves your pity?

Iachimo: Lamentable! What,
To hide me from the radiant sun and solace
I'th' dungeon by a snuff?[3]
Imogen: I pray you, sir,
Deliver with more openness your answers
To my demands. Why do you pity me?

[1] *to be shocked by your husband's behaviour*
[2] *what misfortune do you see in me*
[3] *it's heartbreaking: I can't imagine what it must be like to hide from the sun of true love and find comfort with a prostitute in the dark*

Iachimo now goes even further. If he could experience the love of a beautiful, admirable woman like Imogen, he vows, he would never go astray: how could a man in such a blessed position dishonour himself with common prostitutes in the darkness and squalor of a brothel? He does not name Posthumus, but his meaning is unmistakable.

Imogen is devastated. Iachimo apologises: he had not wished to tell her of Posthumus' shameless promiscuity. As soon as he met Imogen, however, her virtue and nobility made it impossible for him to hide the truth. Now that he knows her, he cannot help but feel pity for her, and is determined to help:

Imogen: My lord, I fear,
Has forgot Britain.
Iachimo: And himself.[1] Not I,
Inclined to this intelligence, pronounce
The beggary of his change,[2] but 'tis your graces
That from my mutest conscience to my tongue
Charms this report out.[3]
Imogen: Let me hear no more.
Iachimo: O dearest soul, your cause doth strike my heart
With pity …

[1] *he has forgotten his better nature; he is no longer himself*
[2] *I take no pleasure in reporting the news of this disgraceful change in him*
[3] *it is your goodness that persuades me to give voice to my innermost thoughts*

Iachimo, sensing Imogen's vulnerability, presses home his point. Posthumus has dishonoured her by mixing with the dregs of Roman society; he is spending his money – most of which he received from the princess – in sordid brothels, sullying the good name of Britain and its royal family. There is only one suitable response: she must take revenge.

Imogen, shocked and confused, still unsure what to believe, asks what he means. Iachimo comes closer. Why should she live a life of self-sacrifice and celibacy, he asks tenderly, while her husband abandons himself to sensual pleasures, at her expense, in Rome? To take her revenge, and for the sake of her own happiness, she deserves a faithful, devoted lover:

Iachimo: I dedicate myself to your sweet pleasure,
More noble than that runagate to your bed,[1]
And will continue fast[2] to your affection,
Still close as sure.[3]

[1] *runaway, fugitive; adulterer*
[2] *constant, loyal*
[3] *forever keeping our love a secret as well as remaining faithful*

The time is right, Iachimo decides, to make his move. He comes closer still, and brings his lips towards hers.

Imogen, suddenly coming to her senses, screams out in alarm. She calls for help, and launches an angry torrent of recrimination at the visitor. His account of Posthumus' behaviour was clearly a pack of lies intended to make her distressed and vulnerable. It is now obvious to her that his only aim was to seduce her, not to pass on genuine information about her husband.

Imogen curses herself for having paid attention to such an impostor. The king will take a very dim view of the newcomer's behaviour, she warns. Iachimo's attempted seduction has failed utterly, and he is in serious trouble.

A gift from France

As Imogen berates him for his blatant attempt to deceive her, Iachimo is forced to think quickly. She has seen through his bid to portray Posthumus as a wild philanderer; he now decides to claim that the whole episode has been an elaborate ploy designed to test Imogen's loyalty. Her angry reaction is proof of her trustworthiness, he explains, and is cause for celebration:

Iachimo: O happy Leonatus![1] I may say
The credit that thy lady hath of thee
Deserves thy trust[2] …
Give me your pardon.
I have spoke this to know if your affiance[3]
Were deeply rooted, and shall make your lord
That which he is new o'er[4] …

1 *fortunate Posthumus*
2 *your wife's belief in your integrity justifies your trust in her*
3 *marriage vows*
4 *when I report your reaction to Posthumus, it will renew and strengthen his standing as your husband*

Imogen responds cautiously; perhaps he is telling the truth. Iachimo becomes even more effusive in his praise of her husband, and finally convinces Imogen that his motives are honourable. Relieved that Posthumus remains true, and cheered by Iachimo's lavish tribute to her husband, she quickly forgets her earlier anger. She welcomes the visitor unreservedly:

Iachimo: He sits 'mongst men like a descended god.
He hath a kind of honour sets him off
More than a mortal seeming.[1] Be not angry,
Most mighty princess, that I have adventured
To try your taking of a false report[2] …
Imogen: All's well, sir. Take my power i'th' court for yours.[3]

1 *that distinguishes him from other men, making him seem greater than a mere mortal*
2 *that I have dared to test your response to a fabricated story about your husband*
3 *you have my authority to do as you wish while at court*

Iachimo has successfully extricated himself from his failed attempt to seduce Imogen, and the atmosphere between the two of them is now cheerful and relaxed.

Iachimo mentions casually that he has a favour to ask. While passing through France on his journey to the British court, he purchased a quantity of beautiful, precious items of gold and silver, as well as some exceptionally fine jewels. This valuable collection is to be a gift to the Roman Emperor; the cost has been shared amongst Iachimo and his friends, including Posthumus. He is naturally concerned to keep the goods safe, and asks Imogen whether she can help. She responds enthusiastically, particularly as the gift is connected with her husband:

Iachimo: … I am something curious, being strange,[1]
To have them in safe stowage. May it please you
To take them in protection?

Imogen: Willingly,
And pawn mine honour for their safety.[2] Since
My lord hath interest[3] in them, I will keep them
In my bedchamber.

[1] *I am rather anxious, as a foreigner*
[2] *I guarantee, on my honour, that they will be safe*
[3] *a stake, a share*

The valuables are in a large trunk, currently guarded by Iachimo's attendants. They will bring it into Imogen's room later, says Iachimo, mentioning that it will only be there for one night; he is leaving tomorrow.

Imogen is disappointed that her husband's friend cannot stay longer. Iachimo apologises; the emperor's gift must be presented very soon, he explains. He has already extended his journey with his brief visit to Britain, which he undertook as a promise to Posthumus. Imogen, grateful that he has gone out of his way, resolves to write a letter for Iachimo to deliver to Posthumus on his return.

A bad loser

Cloten is in an irritable frame of mind. He has just lost a large sum of money in a game of bowls: and to add to his annoyance, he was criticised by a bystander for his foul language. He responded by clouting the man with a bowling ball, but his status as the queen's son made it impossible to challenge him to a duel. This lack of suitable opponents is a constant source of frustration to Cloten. His attendants, while respectful to his face, cannot resist making contemptuous comments behind his back:

Cloten: Would he had been one of my rank.[1]
2nd Lord: [*aside*] To have smelled like a fool.[2]
Cloten: I am not vexed more at anything in th'earth. A pox
on't! I had rather not be so noble as I am. They dare
not fight with me because of the queen my mother.
Every jack-slave hath his bellyful of fighting,[3] and I
must go up and down like a cock that nobody can
match.[4]
2nd Lord: [*aside*] Your are cock and capon,[5] too …

[1] *I wish he had been a nobleman (so that we could have fought a duel)*

[2] *if he had been as rank as you, and of the same status, he would have been a foul-smelling idiot*

[3] *every good-for-nothing rogue can fight to his heart's content*

[4] *like a prize fighting cockerel for which a suitable opponent cannot be found*

[5] *castrated male fowl, considered a symbol of foolishness*

> *"Cloten. What a masterpiece! He deserves more critical attention than he has received as the final distillation of something Shakespeare had been at work on all his life. If Iachimo is his summing up of all that is ungentle in the continental gentleman, so is Cloten of all that is ignoble in the English nobility."*
>
> Harold C. Goddard, *The Meaning of Shakespeare*, 1951

When Cloten hears that there is an Italian visitor at court, he is displeased that he has not been informed. He is even more annoyed when he learns that the man is a friend of Posthumus Leonatus, his rival in love. He wonders for a moment whether it is beneath his dignity to meet this guest, but his attendant assures him sardonically that it is impossible for him to lose his dignity. Cloten, unsure, decides that this is a compliment:

1st Lord:	There's an Italian come, and 'tis thought one of Leonatus' friends.[1]
Cloten:	Leonatus? A banished rascal, and he's another, whatsoever he be[2] ... Is it fit I went to look upon him? Is there no derogation[3] in't?
2nd Lord:	You cannot derogate, my lord.
Cloten:	Not easily, I think.

[1] *he's believed to be a friend of Posthumus*
[2] *whoever this visitor is, he must be a rascal too*
[3] *loss of honour, lowering of status*

Cloten, a keen gambler, decides to pay the Italian a visit. He is confident that he can win enough off the stranger to make up for his earlier loss at bowls.

As Cloten leaves, one of his attendants reflects on his master's stupidity, wondering how an astute, calculating woman like the queen could produce such an oafish son. The fact that he is pursuing Imogen makes her ordeal even worse:

2nd Lord: Alas, poor princess,
Thou divine Imogen, what thou endur'st
Betwixt a father by thy stepdame governed,[1]
A mother hourly coining plots,[2] a wooer
More hateful than the foul expulsion is
Of thy dear husband[3] ...

[1] *dominated by your stepmother, the queen*
[2] *a stepmother who is continually devising plots*
[3] *a suitor who is even more hateful than your husband's banishment*

The attendant prays that Imogen, beset with difficulties as she is, can keep her honour and her sanity. One day, he hopes, she will be reunited with her husband and will regain her rightful status:

2nd Lord: The heavens hold firm
The walls of thy dear honour, keep unshaked[1]
That temple, thy fair mind, that[2] thou mayst stand
T'enjoy thy banished lord and this great land.

[1] *undisturbed, secure*
[2] *so that*

An intruder

II, ii

It is midnight, and Imogen is in bed. She has been reading for three hours, and is now weary and ready for sleep. She hands her book to Helen, her maidservant, and asks her to fold down the page to mark her place. Helen then leaves, and Imogen says a brief prayer to the gods:

Imogen: To your protection I commend me, gods.
From fairies and the tempters of the night,[1]
Guard me, beseech ye.[2]

[1] *sinister supernatural beings and evil spirits*
[2] *I pray, I beg you*

The princess lies down and quickly drifts off to sleep, her bedchamber lit by a solitary candle. In the stillness, the only sound that can be heard is the quiet chirping of crickets outside her window.

Imogen is not alone, however. Near her bed is the trunk belonging to the Italian visitor, placed in her bedchamber for safe keeping. The lid of the trunk – which supposedly contained precious gifts for the Roman Emperor – now opens, and Iachimo himself cautiously emerges.

Pen and paper in hand, the intruder aims to record every last detail of the room. As his attempt to seduce Imogen has failed, he must fabricate evidence that he has spent the night with her if he is to win his wager with Posthumus. He is distracted from his objective, however, when his first sight of the sleeping Imogen fills him with longing:

Iachimo: … How bravely thou becom'st thy bed! [1] Fresh lily,
And whiter than the sheets! That I might touch,
But kiss, one kiss. Rubies unparagoned,
How dearly they do't.[2] 'Tis her breathing that
Perfumes the chamber thus.

[1] *how finely you adorn your bed*
[2] *how exquisitely your lips, like matchless rubies, kiss one another*

Forcing himself to concentrate on the task at hand, Iachimo starts to note down the various pictures, tapestries and furnishings that the bedchamber contains. Quickly realising that some distinctive feature of Imogen's body would provide far more convincing proof, he approaches the sleeping figure in the bed.

As he comes nearer, Iachimo notices a bracelet on the princess's bare arm. He carefully slides it off; it will help to convince Posthumus of his success. Now that he is close to her, he notices a detail that will surely put his claim beyond doubt:

Iachimo: On her left breast
A mole, cinque-spotted,[1] like the crimson drops
I'th' bottom of a cowslip. Here's a voucher
Stronger than ever law could make;[2] this secret
Will force him think I have picked the lock and ta'en
The treasure of her honour.[3]

[1] *made up of five separate spots*
[2] *a piece of evidence more powerful than any that a lawyer could produce*
[3] *compel him to believe that I have seduced her*

There is no need to write anything else down: the vision of Imogen's body is fixed indelibly in his memory.

> *... A mole, cinque-spotted, like the crimson drops*
> *I'th' bottom of a cowslip.*
>
> *"The audience is forced to confront its own complicity in Iachimo's deed. His gaze is ours."*
>
> Jonathan Bate and Will Sharpe, Introduction to the RSC Shakespeare edition of *Cymbeline*, 2011

Iachimo reminds himself that, as an intruder in the princess's bedchamber, he is in mortal danger. Dawn is not far off, and he creeps hurriedly back into the trunk:

Iachimo: I lodge in fear;
Though this[1] a heavenly angel, hell is here.
[*a clock strikes*] One, two, three: time, time.

[1] *Imogen is*

Music at dawn

II, iii

It is now early morning, and Cloten has been gambling all night. He has lost heavily, and is in low spirits. If he succeeds in marrying the princess, he remarks, his money worries will be over. As part of his campaign to win Imogen's love, it has been suggested that music should be played outside her bedchamber in the mornings. The musicians now arrive, and Cloten urges them to prepare. With the seduction of Imogen in mind, he cannot resist some obscene wordplay:

Cloten: ... I am advised to give her music o' mornings; they say it will penetrate.[1]
[*the musicians arrive*]
Come on, tune.[2] If you can penetrate her with your fingering, so;[3] we'll try with tongue, too. If none will do, let her remain, but I'll never give o'er.[4]

[1] *influence her, get through to her*
[2] *tune up, get ready to play*
[3] *so much the better*
[4] *If we don't succeed, she can stay as she is, but I'll never give up*

The musicians' song, in contrast to Cloten's boorish manner, is a courtly, delicate call to greet the new day:

Hark, hark, the lark at heaven's gate sings,
    And Phoebus 'gins arise,[1]
His steeds to water at those springs
    On chaliced flowers that lies,[2]
And winking Mary-buds begin to ope their golden eyes.[3]
With every thing that pretty is, my lady sweet, arise,
    Arise, arise.

[1] *the sun god is beginning to rise*
[2] *to allow his horses to drink the dew from cupped flowers*
[3] *sleeping marigolds begin to unfurl their petals*

The musicians leave. Cloten waits expectantly outside Imogen's room, but there is no response. When Cymbeline and the queen approach he states, bluntly, that the music does not seem to be working. The king reassures him that the princess will eventually change her mind. For the time being, the banished Posthumus is still on her mind:

Cymbeline: Attend you here the door of our stern daughter?[1]
Will she not forth?
Cloten: I have assailed her with musics, but she vouchsafes no notice.[2]
Cymbeline: The exile of her minion[3] is too new.
She hath not yet forgot him. Some more time
Must wear the print of his remembrance out,[4]
And then she's yours.

[1] *are you waiting for my hard-hearted daughter?*
[2] *I have bombarded her with music and songs, but she does not deign to respond*
[3] *darling, sweetheart*
[4] *erase the memory of Posthumus from her mind*

The queen, too, encourages her son not to lose heart. He must be more devoted and persistent, she advises him, and faithfully obey Imogen's every wish, unless her wish is to be left alone. Her words are wasted, however, on the dim-witted Cloten:

Queen: … so seem as if
You were inspired to do those duties which
You tender to her,[1] that you in all obey her,
Save when command to your dismission tends,
And therein you are senseless.[2]
Cloten: Senseless?[3] Not so.

[1] *when you offer to be of service to her, make it appear that your feelings are genuine and enthusiastic*
[2] *obey her in everything, except when she orders you to go away, in which case you must remain oblivious*
[3] *misinterpreted as meaning 'stupid'*

A messenger now enters with news for the king: Caius Lucius, an important ambassador from Rome, has just arrived. Cymbeline knows and respects the man, although he suspects that the message he brings from Augustus Caesar will be a hostile one. He leaves, with the queen, to greet the ambassador.

Cloten is now alone outside Imogen's door. Although she has not responded to his music, he resolves to speak to her.

An unwanted admirer

Cloten knocks at Imogen's door. He is aware that he will not be welcome, and decides to bribe her maidservant, Dorothy, to bring him into the princess's company:

Dorothy: … What's your lordship's pleasure?
Cloten: Your lady's person.[1] Is she ready?
Dorothy: Ay,
To keep her chamber.[2]
Cloten: There is gold for you.
Sell me your good report.[3]

[1] *presence; body*
[2] *yes; she is ready to remain in her room*
[3] *in return, speak well of me to Imogen*

Just as Dorothy leaves, Imogen herself appears at the door. She immediately makes it clear that Cloten's feelings, whether they are genuine or not, are of no interest to her:

Cloten: … I swear I love you.
Imogen: If you but said so, 'twere as deep with me;[1]
If you swear still, your recompense is still
That I regard it not.[2]

[1] *it makes no difference to me whether you swear it or just say it*
[2] *if you swear continually that you love me, your reward will continually be that I take no notice*

She is only talking to Cloten, explains Imogen, because her silence might be mistaken for approval. She wants to make it absolutely clear how much she dislikes him; indeed, her feelings of revulsion are so strong that she feels uncomfortable putting them into words. Cloten rebukes her for her wilfulness:

Imogen: I care not for you,
And am so near the lack of charity
To accuse myself I hate you,[1] which I had rather
You felt than make't my boast.[2]
Cloten: You sin against
Obedience, which you owe your father.

[1] *I am so close to lacking proper Christian charity that I could almost accuse myself of hating you*
[2] *I wish you could grasp how much I dislike you without my having to spell it out*

Cloten, offended, now pours scorn on Imogen's choice of husband. As an orphan and a commoner, Posthumus is utterly unfit to partner a princess, and their marriage vows cannot be considered valid:

Cloten: … The contract you pretend[1] with that base wretch,
One bred of alms and fostered with cold dishes,
With scraps o'th' court,[2] it is no contract, none …

[1] *as for the marriage contract you claim to have entered into*
[2] *brought up on charity, and fed with the court's leftovers*

Imogen can no longer contain her fury. In her eyes, Posthumus is infinitely more noble than Cloten:

Imogen: He never can meet more mischance than come
To be but named of thee.[1] His meanest garment
That ever hath but clipped his body[2] is dearer
In my respect than all the hairs above thee,
Were they all made such men.[3]

[1] *simply being mentioned by you is the worst thing that could happen to him*
[2] *the most worthless item of clothing that he has ever worn*
[3] *than all the hairs on your head, if they were turned into men like you*

At this point, Imogen's attention is diverted, and she calls for her servant Pisanio. On top of the distress caused by her unwelcome guest, she has suddenly become aware that her bracelet, a parting gift from Posthumus, is no longer on her arm:

Imogen: [*to Pisanio*] I am sprited with a fool,
Frighted and angered worse.[1] Go bid my woman
Search for a jewel that too casually
Hath left mine arm; it was thy master's. 'Shrew me[2]
If I would lose it for a revenue[3]
Of any king's in Europe.

[1] *I am being haunted by a foolish spirit that is both frightening me and, worse, making me angry*
[2] *the devil take me*
[3] *the wealth*

Pisanio, reassuring his mistress that the bracelet will be found, hurries away to alert Imogen's maidservant.

Cloten, meanwhile, is still brooding over the princess's insult, and her scornful comparison between Posthumus and himself. He becomes threatening, but Imogen has by now lost interest in the quarrel. She goes back into her room, shutting the door in Cloten's face:

Cloten: You have abused[1] me.
His meanest garment?
Imogen: Ay, I said so, sir.
If you will make't an action, call witness to't.[2]
Cloten: I will inform your father.
Imogen: Your mother, too.
She's my good lady and will conceive, I hope,
But the worst of me.[3] So I leave you, sir,
To th'worst of discontent.
Cloten: I'll be revenged.
His meanest garment? Well.

1 *insulted, offended*
2 *if you want to sue me, call a witness to support your case*
3 *I'm confident that she will disapprove*

An ultimatum

II, iv

Back in Rome, Philario and Posthumus are in conversation. Posthumus expresses the hope that Cymbeline will, one day, allow him to return to Britain. For the time being, he can do nothing but wait, and he is greatly indebted to Philario for his hospitality.

Although the two men are firm friends, relations between their respective homelands are increasingly hostile. In previous military encounters, troops of the Roman Empire have subdued Britain; and in return for peaceful co-existence, Rome has demanded regular payments, known as tribute, from the defeated Britons.

For some time now, Cymbeline has failed to pay the required tribute. In response, the Roman Emperor has sent his ambassador, Caius Lucius, to Britain to deliver a stark warning: if the tribute is not paid, invasion will follow. Philario is confident that the tribute will be paid in full, as Britons must remember only too well their earlier bloody clashes with Rome. Posthumus, convinced that Britain will choose to fight, disagrees:

Philario: … I think
He'll grant the tribute, send th'arrearages,[1]
Or look upon our Romans, whose remembrance
Is yet fresh in their grief.[2]

Posthumus: I do believe –
Statist though I am none, nor like to be[3] –
That this will prove a war; and you shall hear
The legions now in Gallia sooner landed
In our not-fearing Britain than have tidings
Of any penny tribute paid.[4]

[1] *Cymbeline will pay the tribute, including all amounts that are overdue*

[2] *face the Roman army, the memory of which is still a source of grief and fear to the Britons*

[3] *although I am not a politician, nor likely to become one*

[4] *you will hear news that the Roman troops stationed in France have landed in fearless Britain sooner than you hear of any tribute being paid*

At the time of the earlier invasions, Posthumus believes, Britain's forces, though brave, were unprepared and disorganised. If Rome attempts another invasion, it will face a much more skilful, disciplined army.

Cymbeline is set in ancient Britain in the early days of the Roman Empire, although the play's events and characters are largely fictional. At this time, Britain was not under Roman occupation, although it was strongly influenced by Rome; the empire extended as far as Gaul, only twenty miles away across the English Channel.

Earlier attempts by Julius Caesar to invade Britain had only been partially successful. A number of important hostages had been taken and, as mentioned in the play, it was agreed that Britain should pay an annual sum in tribute to Rome.

Shakespeare's audience would have been aware that, nearly fifty years later, there was to be another invasion, ordered by the emperor Claudius, which would result in the eventual conquest of Britain and the creation of the Roman province of Britannia. After this, the Roman occupation would continue for over three hundred years:

"Shakespeare's Cymbeline *is set in this transitional period – the last decades of the free British. It explores the uneasy relationships between the British aristocracy and Rome, and the internal tension which there would inevitably have been between those who saw Rome as a hated enemy and those who believed that in Rome lay the future."*

Barry Cunliffe, Programme notes for the RSC production of *Cymbeline*, 1989

A persuasive story

The discussion is interrupted by the arrival of a visitor: Iachimo, after his brief sojourn in Britain, has returned.

Posthumus' mind turns immediately to his wager. Iachimo's swift return, he suggests, demonstrates how quickly and totally Imogen has rejected him. Iachimo, by contrast, does not approach the subject directly:

Posthumus: I hope the briefness of your answer[1] made
The speediness of your return.

Iachimo: Your lady
Is one of the fairest that I have looked upon.

[1] *Imogen's quick, dismissive response to you*

Iachimo, in no hurry to discuss his visit, casually hands Posthumus some letters from Britain. He mentions to Philario that, at the time of his stay, the ambassador from Rome had not yet arrived, although he was expected very shortly. Posthumus interrupts: having read the letters, he is keen to come back to the subject of their wager.

The two men had agreed that if Iachimo succeeded in seducing Imogen, Posthumus would hand over his diamond ring. He has clearly failed, says Posthumus mockingly, and the ring – like Imogen – remains out of his grasp. He dismisses Iachimo's implication that he has been successful, and reminds him that their friendship must come to an end immediately. Iachimo's insult to his wife's honour is clearly unjustified, and is a serious matter:

Iachimo: I'll make a journey twice as far t'enjoy
A second night of such sweet shortness which
Was mine in Britain, for the ring is won.
Posthumus: The stone's too hard to come by.[1]
Iachimo: Not a whit,
Your lady being so easy.[2]
Posthumus: Make not, sir,
Your loss your sport.[3] I hope you know that we
Must not continue friends.

[1] *winning this diamond has proved too hard a task for you*
[2] *not at all, as it proved so easy to seduce Imogen*
[3] *don't make a joke out of the fact that you have lost*

Iachimo persists: he has slept with Imogen, and, as agreed, wins Posthumus' ring. He has not made any false claims, he points out calmly, so there is no need for the two of them to become enemies.

Posthumus, provoked almost beyond endurance, demands that Iachimo provide evidence for his hateful assertions. This has become a matter of life and death:

Posthumus: If you can make't apparent[1]
That you have tasted her in bed, my hand
And ring is yours.[2] If not, the foul opinion
You had of her pure honour gains or loses
Your sword or mine, or masterless leaves both
To who shall find them.[3]

[1] *demonstrate, prove*
[2] *I will shake your hand and give you my ring*
[3] *means that we must fight a duel; one of us will kill the other, gaining his sword, or we may both die*

Iachimo, unruffled, states that he will give Posthumus all the proof he requires. He starts by describing Imogen's room:

Iachimo: First, her bedchamber –
Where I confess I slept not, but profess
Had that was well worth watching[1] – it was hanged
With tapestry of silk and silver, the story[2]
Proud Cleopatra when she met her Roman[3] …

[1] *what I experienced was well worth staying awake for*
[2] *depicting*
[3] *Mark Antony, her future lover*

Iachimo continues, recalling every item in the room in loving detail. Posthumus remains calm. Perhaps someone has described the room to him; perhaps Iachimo even visited the room himself. He clearly has a good memory, says Posthumus mockingly, but nothing Iachimo has said suggests that he has been successful in his plan to seduce Imogen.

Posthumus is shaken to the core, however, when the next piece of evidence is presented to him. For a brief, tantalising moment, Iachimo reveals the bracelet that he slipped off Imogen's arm as she slept. Perhaps the bracelet and ring are a matching pair, he suggests airily; in any case, they are both his now, as he has won the wager.

Posthumus demands to see the bracelet again. Wracked with anxiety, he asks whether it is the one that he gave Imogen when they parted. Iachimo confirms his worst fears:

Posthumus: Jove!
Once more let me behold it. Is it that
Which I left with her?
Iachimo: Sir, I thank her, that.[1]
She stripped it from her arm. I see her yet.
Her pretty action did outsell her gift,[2]
And yet enriched it, too. She gave it me,
And said she prized it once.

[1] *that's right, and I'm grateful to Imogen for the gift*
[2] *her sweet gesture was more precious to me than the bracelet itself*

Regaining his composure, Posthumus tries to think of an explanation; perhaps she gave the bracelet to Iachimo to pass on to him? Iachimo asks pointedly whether she mentioned this in the letter that Posthumus has just read.

Both men, of course, know that this is not the case; and Posthumus, utterly defeated, realises that there is only one possible conclusion: his wife has been unfaithful. Iachimo has seduced her, just as he boasted he would. Posthumus hands the ring to his rival, bitterly lamenting the deceitfulness and disloyalty of beautiful women such as Imogen.

> *"Iachimo epitomises everything Elizabethans had heard or imagined about super-subtle Italians. He is an artist in evil-doing, as wholly intellectual in his vice as Cloten is animal."*
>
> Anne Barton, Programme notes for the RSC production of *Cymbeline*, 1974

Conclusive proof

Philario, alarmed to see his guest in such distress, now intervenes. Iachimo's story may not be true: perhaps Imogen simply lost the bracelet, he suggests, or one of her servants may have been bribed to steal it from her. Posthumus, relieved, realises that he may have been too hasty, and he takes back the ring.

Posthumus' relief, however, is short-lived. A simple declaration by Iachimo is enough to convince him that there can be no other explanation for the loss of Imogen's bracelet. Once again he hands over the ring, cursing both Imogen and her seducer:

Iachimo: By Jupiter, I had it from her arm.
Posthumus: Hark you, he swears; by Jupiter he swears.
'Tis true, nay, keep the ring; 'tis true. I am sure
She would not lose it. Her attendants are
All sworn and honourable. They induced to steal it?
And by a stranger? No, he hath enjoyed her.[1]
[*he gives Iachimo the ring again*]
... There, take thy hire,[2] and all the fiends of hell
Divide themselves between you![3]

[1] *enjoyed her body, seduced her*
[2] *fee, reward*
[3] *between Iachimo and Imogen*

Philario again tries to placate his friend, but Posthumus brushes aside his well-meaning remarks. The image of Iachimo making love to Imogen is now fixed indelibly in his mind:

Philario: Sir, be patient.
This is not strong enough to be believed
Of one persuaded well of.[1]
Posthumus: Never talk on't.
She hath been colted[2] by him.

[1] *about someone highly thought of, like Imogen*
[2] *mounted, as if by a lusty young animal*

Iachimo, sensing Posthumus' vulnerability, decides that now is the time to put the matter beyond doubt:

Iachimo: If you seek
For further satisfying, under her breast –
Worthy the pressing[1] – lies a mole, right proud
Of that most delicate lodging. By my life
I kissed it, and it gave me present hunger
To feed again, though full.[2] You do remember
This stain upon her?
Posthumus: Ay, and it doth confirm
Another stain,[3] as big as hell can hold ...

[1] *which I found worth caressing*
[2] *it immediately made me hungry for more, even though I had had my fill*
[3] *it is a sign of a far greater moral blemish*

Iachimo volunteers to provide even more information, and to declare under oath that he is telling the truth. However, Posthumus, already tormented beyond endurance, refuses to listen. He now has only one desire: to take violent revenge on his adulterous wife. Almost incoherent with rage, he storms out, vowing to set off for Britain at once:

Posthumus: O that I had her here to tear her limb-meal![1]
I will go there and do't i'th' court, before
Her father. I'll do something – [*he leaves*]
Philario: Quite besides
The government of patience.[2]

[1] *I wish she were here so that I could tear her limb from limb*
[2] *he is no longer governed by his patience; he has lost his self-control*

Philario concedes that Iachimo has won his bet; for the present, however, his concern is for his guest's sanity and safety. He hurries away after Posthumus. Iachimo, with a display of sympathy, follows.

A violent reaction

Posthumus, now alone, is agonising over Imogen's disloyalty. His rage has subsided, leaving a bitter, all-consuming hatred, not only for his wife but for women in general. He is convinced that women are inherently untrustworthy. His own mother, who died giving birth to him, had a reputation for purity and virtue; but she, like Imogen, was undoubtedly as fickle and adulterous as the rest. The identity of his true father will never be known:

Posthumus: We are all bastards,
And that most venerable man which I
Did call my father was I know not where
When I was stamped.[1] Some coiner with his tools
Made me a counterfeit;[2] yet my mother seemed
The Dian[3] of that time, so doth my wife
The nonpareil of this.[4]

[1] *created; conceived*
[2] *I am illegitimate, like a counterfeit coin produced by a forger*
[3] *Diana, the goddess associated with modesty and chastity*
[4] *in the same way, my wife is now considered to be of unequalled merit*

Posthumus' revulsion grows as, in his mind's eye, he dwells obsessively on the scene in Imogen's bedchamber as she submits willingly to the lustful visitor. But infidelity is not womankind's only fault: women are the source of all the world's evils, he decides. Even in men, wrongdoing is the result of the malignant influence of women, whether inherited through the generations or spread like a contagion:

Posthumus: ... there's no motion
That tends to vice in man but I affirm
It is the woman's part:[1] be it lying, note it,
The woman's; flattering, hers; deceiving, hers;
Lust and rank thoughts, hers, hers; revenges, hers;
Ambitions, covetings, change of prides,[2] disdain,
Nice-longing,[3] slanders, mutability,[4]

All faults that may be named, nay, that hell knows,
Why hers, in part or all …

[1] *every impulse that leads to wickedness in men is derived from women*
[2] *continual turning from one excess to another*
[3] *lascivious desire*
[4] *unreliability, fickleness*

As his resentment grows, Posthumus becomes consumed by one overriding thought: Imogen must be made to pay for her treachery.

Several of Shakespeare's plays feature women, like Imogen in *Cymbeline*, who have been unjustly slandered. Victims of defamation of this kind often took their complaints to a consistory court (a court presided over by church officials); as these courts dealt with a large number of cases involving fornication, adultery, illegitimate births and sexual slander, they were commonly known as 'bawdy courts'.

Towards the end of Shakespeare's career, his own family was involved in such a dispute. His daughter Susanna, who in 1607 had married a highly respected doctor, John Hall, won her case against an accuser who was notorious for slander, rioting and drunkenness:

"… in an irony that cannot have been lost on Shakespeare, in 1613, after he had written five plays that turn on the slander of a woman, Susanna Shakespeare Hall was publicly accused of adultery and having a venereal disease by a man named John Lane. Given the need to defend her reputation, Susanna sued her accuser in the consistory court of Worcester Cathedral, and won the case when Lane did not appear."

Valerie Wayne, Introduction to the Arden Shakespeare edition of *Cymbeline*, 2017

War is declared

At the British court, an important summit is taking place. Caius Lucius, the ambassador from Rome, has come with a message from the emperor, Augustus Caesar. Facing Lucius is Cymbeline, with the queen and her son at his side.

Lucius reminds Cymbeline that Augustus' predecessor, the renowned Julius Caesar, invaded Britain many years ago. The British ruler at that time agreed to pay, in return for peace and independence, an annual tribute of three thousand pounds. Despite reminders, states Lucius, the sum has not been paid in recent years. The queen and her son both respond swiftly and defiantly. The country has a natural right to its independence, Cloten declares, and no further tribute will be paid:

Cloten: There be many Caesars,
Ere such another Julius.[1] Britain's a world
By itself, and we will nothing pay
For wearing our own noses.[2]

[1] *before there is another like Julius Caesar*
[2] *for being ourselves (Romans supposedly had large, prominent noses)*

The queen points out that Julius Caesar's victory was far from easy. The stormy seas surrounding Britain provide effective protection and, for the first time in his career, Caesar had been forced to admit defeat in his initial attempts to invade the country:

Queen: A kind of conquest
Caesar made here, but made not here his brag
Of 'came and saw and overcame'.[1] With shame –
The first that ever touched him – he was carried
From off our coast, twice beaten, and his shipping,
Poor ignorant baubles,[2] on our terrible seas
Like eggshells moved upon their surges, cracked
As easily 'gainst our rocks.[3]

[1] *his boast of 'veni, vidi, vici' (I came, I saw, I conquered) was not made about Britain*
[2] *flimsy vessels not built for rough seas*
[3] *were dragged along by the waves and smashed against the rocky shores like eggshells*

In Shakespeare's time, the word 'Britain' was generally used only to refer to the ancient land of warring tribes and mythical kings. The word was given new life, however, by King James, who had succeeded Queen Elizabeth; as king of both Scotland and England, he was determined to unite the two nations politically into a single country, and he encouraged the use of the word 'Britain'. He liked to refer to himself as 'King of Great Britain', even though the phrase had no legal or constitutional meaning.

The new king – patron of Shakespeare's theatre company – had come to the throne about five years before Shakespeare wrote *Cymbeline*. In this play, was Shakespeare showing sympathy for the monarch's ambition to unite the two kingdoms?

"In the history plays, written in the 1590s, Shakespeare always refers to his own country as England ... Elizabethan Shakespeare, in short, was an English dramatist. Jacobean Shakespeare, by contrast, was a British one; Jacobean Shakespeare was a dramatist who spoke openly in favour of his royal patron's project to create (or re-create) a kingdom of Britain. In Cymbeline, *written for the court of King James, he used either 'Britain' to mean his country or 'Britons' for its people nearly fifty times."*

Jonathan Bate, *Soul of the Age*, 2008

Cymbeline now adds his voice. Britain was a free kingdom before the arrival of the Romans, he states, and it is only to be expected that the country will resist the demands of Rome. Lucius announces, regretfully, that it is his duty to inform Cymbeline that hostile military action will follow:

Lucius: I am sorry, Cymbeline,
That I am to pronounce Augustus Caesar –
Caesar that hath more kings his servants than
Thyself domestic officers[1] – thine enemy.
Receive it from me then: war and confusion
In Caesar's name pronounce I 'gainst thee.

[1] *who has more kings as his servants than you have household attendants*

Despite the nature of their exchanges, the two men remain calm and amicable. Cymbeline has spent time in Rome, and feels no animosity towards Augustus. However, he is aware that other nations are currently resisting the might of Rome, and it would show weakness if Britain did not do the same. If Augustus attempts an invasion, he will meet fierce opposition. Lucius does not argue with Cymbeline: he replies, diplomatically, that events will have to speak for themselves.

Duplicity

III, ii

Elsewhere in the British court, Pisanio has just received a letter from his master Posthumus. He is astonished and horrified at its contents. Someone in Rome has clearly misled Posthumus into believing that his wife has been unfaithful:

Pisanio: How? Of adultery? Wherefore write you not
What monster's her accuser?[1] Leonatus,
O master, what a strange infection
Is fall'n into thy ear? What false Italian,
As poisonous tongued as handed,[2] hath prevailed
On thy too ready hearing? Disloyal? No.

[1] *why have you not named the villain who accused her?*
[2] *ready both to administer poison and to spread poisonous lies*

It is inconceivable that Imogen should be untrue to her husband: indeed, it is her loyalty to him that is the cause of her present suffering. But Posthumus has gone even further. In the letter, he instructs Pisanio, bluntly, to murder Imogen. He has enclosed a second letter, to be read by her, which will assist Pisanio in his task.

Pisanio is appalled at his master's cruel and irrational command. When Imogen herself approaches, he hands her the second letter, but resolves to say nothing about the shocking message that he has just read.

Imogen is joyful and excited to hear from her husband. She recognises the familiar handwriting, and prays that the letter will contain good news:

Imogen: O, learn'd indeed were that astronomer
That knew the stars as I his characters:
He'd lay the future open.[1] You good gods,
Let what is here contained relish of love,[2]
Of my lord's health, of his content[3] ...

[1] *an astrologer who knew the stars as I well as I know Posthumus' writing could easily predict the future*
[2] *may the contents of this letter taste of love*
[3] *happiness*

Imogen opens the letter. The message is brief and enigmatic, but its meaning is clear. Posthumus has, unexpectedly, returned from exile:

... Take notice that I am in Cambria[1] at Milford Haven. What your own love will out of this advise you, follow. So he wishes you all happiness that remains loyal to his vow, and your increasing in love, Leonatus Posthumus.

[1] *Wales*

Beside herself with excitement, Imogen intends to set out for Milford Haven without delay to meet her beloved. She questions Pisanio impatiently about the journey:

Imogen: O for a horse with wings! Hear'st thou, Pisanio?
He is at Milford Haven! Read and tell me
How far 'tis thither. If one of mean affairs[1]
May plod it in a week, why may not I
Glide thither in a day?

[1] *travelling on unimportant business*

As Imogen considers the sudden, unexpected news, an outpouring of thoughts and questions follows. How can she slip away from court unseen? And even if she makes no more than a brief visit to Milford Haven, how will she account for her absence? Shrugging off these questions for the present, she asks Pisanio again how quickly they can travel:

Imogen: Prithee speak,
How many score[1] of miles may we well ride
'Twixt hour and hour? [2]
Pisanio: One score 'twixt sun and sun,[3]
Madam, 's enough for you, and too much too.
Imogen: Why, one that rode to's execution, man,
Could never go so slow.

[1] *lots of twenty*
[2] *in the space of an hour*
[3] *just twenty in the space of a day*

Cheerfully dismissing Pisanio's cautious answer, Imogen decides that the length of the journey is irrelevant; she is going anyway, regardless of the distance, and Pisanio will accompany her. First, he is to persuade her maidservant to feign illness and leave the court, so that Imogen's departure will not be witnessed. Then, he must bring Imogen some plain, inexpensive riding-clothes to ensure that her royal status does not attract attention during the journey.

Pisanio is hesitant; he is aware that Imogen's husband, in truth, is not at Milford Haven. However, he cannot reveal the terrible contents of his own letter from Posthumus, so he has no choice but to go along with his mistress's plan.

A change of scene

III, iii

In the depths of rural Wales, on a wild, remote, wooded mountainside, the elderly Belarius emerges from the mouth of a cave. He calls out to two youths within the cave to come out and greet the new day.

As the young men emerge, crouching under the low gateway, he points out that the cave's low ceiling forces them to show reverence and humility. The dwellings of the wealthy and powerful, by contrast, encourage no such respect for the powers above:

Belarius: Stoop, boys: this gate
Instructs you how t'adore the heavens, and bows you
To a morning's holy office.[1] The gates of monarchs
Are arched so high that giants may jet[2] through
And keep their impious turbans on without
Good morrow to the sun.

[1] *makes you bow down, to take part in your morning's religious observances*
[2] *strut proudly*

It quickly becomes clear that Belarius has not always lived in these lonely, austere surroundings; he has also experienced the very different life of a courtier. He is not nostalgic about those earlier years, however, and is keen to impress on the two young men the advantages of their present life:

Belarius: O, this life
Is nobler than attending for a check,[1]
Richer than doing nothing for a bauble,[2]
Prouder than rustling in unpaid-for silk[3] …

[1] *waiting on your superiors, only to be rewarded with a rebuke*
[2] *carrying out pointless tasks for a trivial reward*
[3] *wearing fine clothes obtained on credit*

Guiderius, the older of the two youths, is not convinced. After all, he and his brother Arviragus have never known any life but this, and they are becoming impatient to experience the wider world:

Guiderius: Haply[1] this life is best,
If quiet life be best, sweeter to you
That have a sharper known, well corresponding
With your stiff age.[2] But unto us it is
A cell of ignorance, travelling abed[3] …

[1] *perhaps*
[2] *you find it pleasant as you have had experience of a more difficult life, and it suits you now that you are older and set in your ways*
[3] *this life keeps us confined in ignorance, and we can only travel in our dreams*

Arviragus adds his voice. The thought of spending the rest of their lives in these wild, secluded surroundings is intolerable. He foresees a bleak, cheerless future for himself and his brother:

Arviragus: What should we speak of
When we are old as you? When we shall hear
The rain and wind beat dark December,[1] how
In this our pinching[2] cave shall we discourse
The freezing hours away? We have seen nothing:
We are beastly[3] …

[1] *beat down, marking the ominous arrival of December*
[2] *narrow, restrictive; bitingly cold*
[3] *no better than beasts*

When we shall hear
The rain and wind beat dark December …

"This powerful speech is a reminder that the countryside of this play is no utopia; it is far removed from the idealized landscape of literary pastoral. In the harsh winter weather there can be no pretending: here people are forced to come to terms with themselves and others …"

Roger Warren, Introduction to the Oxford Shakespeare edition of *Cymbeline*, 1998

Their only skill is hunting for food, Arviragus complains, which involves cunning but no courage. Any pleasure they take from life must be within the confines of their harsh, isolated existence:

Arviragus: Our valour is to chase what flies;[1] our cage
We make a choir,[2] as doth the prisoned bird,
And sing our bondage freely.[3]

[1] *the only courage we can demonstrate is to chase animals that are trying to escape from us*
[2] *we make our restricted surroundings a place to sing*
[3] *the only thing we can sing about freely is our captivity*

Belarius rebukes the young men sternly; if only they knew what life at court was really like, with its malice, dishonesty and ingratitude, they would show more appreciation for their life out in the wilderness. He reminds them that he was once a favourite at Cymbeline's court, renowned for his courage in resisting the Roman invaders:

Belarius: … my body's marked
With Roman swords, and my report was once
First with the best of note.[1] Cymbeline loved me,
And when a soldier was the theme, my name
Was not far off.[2]

[1] *my reputation was supreme among the most distinguished individuals*
[2] *whenever people talked of military matters, it was not long before my name was mentioned*

All it took to destroy his good name, Belarius recalls, was a spiteful, unfounded rumour:

Belarius: … two villains, whose false oaths prevailed
Before my perfect[1] honour, swore to Cymbeline
I was confederate[2] with the Romans. So
Followed my banishment, and this twenty years
This rock and these demesnes[3] have been my world,
Where I have lived at honest freedom …

[1] *unblemished*
[2] *collaborating, conspiring*
[3] *territories*

A long-kept secret

Belarius sends Guiderius and Arviragus into the mountains to hunt for food. Once alone, he reflects on the truth that he has kept hidden for the last twenty years: the two young men, though they do not realise it, are the sons of Cymbeline, king of Britain. Despite their lowly upbringing in these harsh, inhospitable surroundings, they have a natural nobility which cannot be suppressed:

Belarius: How hard it is to hide the sparks of nature!
These boys know little they are sons to th' king,
Nor Cymbeline dreams that they are alive.
They think they are mine, and though trained up thus meanly [1]
I'th' cave wherein they bow, their thoughts do hit
The roofs of palaces [2] …

[1] *raised in such lowly circumstances*
[2] *are lofty and majestic*

As far as the boys are concerned, their names are Polydore and Cadwal, and the cramped cave in the Welsh mountains has always been their home. They believe that the man who has brought them up – known to them as Morgan – is their father.

The truth, however, is very different; Belarius in fact stole them away from Cymbeline when they were infants, as an act of revenge for his wrongful banishment. At that time the two boys were the king's only children:

Belarius: O Cymbeline, heaven and my conscience knows
Thou didst unjustly banish me, whereon
At three and two years old I stole these babes,
Thinking to bar thee of succession, as
Thou reft'st me of my lands.[1]

[1] *aiming to deprive you of heirs, just as you robbed me of my home*

Belarius had persuaded Euriphile, the boys' nurse, to help him; and the two of them secretly fled the court together, taking Guiderius and Arviragus with them. As the children grew up, they assumed that Euriphile was their mother. She has since died, but is not forgotten:

Belarius: Euriphile,
Thou wast their nurse; they took thee for their mother,
And every day do honour to her grave.

Devastating news III, iv

Having slipped away from court, Imogen is on her way to Milford Haven, accompanied by the faithful Pisanio, to be reunited with her husband. She is becoming impatient; they dismounted from their horses some time ago, and Pisanio reassured her that it was just a short walk to Milford Haven, where they would find Posthumus.

Imogen is concerned to see that Pisanio has a look of unbearable anguish on his face. He can no longer hide the terrible truth about Posthumus, but he cannot bring himself to tell his mistress directly. Instead, he wordlessly hands her the letter that he received from her husband. Imogen reads with growing horror:

Thy mistress, Pisanio, hath played the strumpet[1] *in my bed ... I speak not out of weak surmises,*[2] *but from proof as strong as my grief, and as certain as I expect my revenge. That part thou, Pisanio, must act for me ... Let thine own hands take away her life.*

[1] *behaved like a whore*
[2] *uninformed guesses*

The letter explains how Posthumus has deliberately lured Imogen away from court by claiming that he has returned from exile: this will make it easier for Pisanio to dispose of her, as there will be no witnesses or other complications.

If Pisanio is truly his loyal servant, writes Posthumus, he will carry out the deed and send proof of his success back to Rome:

> *... if thou fear to strike and to make me certain it is done, thou art the pander to her dishonour*[1] *and equally to me disloyal.*
>
> [1] *you will be colluding in her infidelity*

Pisanio looks on as Imogen reads. Her overwhelming grief is obvious:

Pisanio: What[1] shall I need to draw my sword? The paper
Hath cut her throat already.

[1] *why*

Imogen is utterly bewildered at the idea that she could be unfaithful to her beloved husband. Then she suddenly remembers the strange incident with the Italian visitor, Iachimo, who pretended briefly that Posthumus was living a life of debauchery in Rome. Perhaps it was not a pretence after all; perhaps Posthumus has been led astray by a seductive Roman courtesan, and now wants his wife out of the way. She curses herself for believing his declarations of love:

Imogen: Some jay[1] of Italy,
Whose mother was her painting,[2] hath betrayed him.[3]
Poor I am stale,[4] a garment out of fashion …
… O,
Men's vows are women's traitors.

[1] *gaudily dressed prostitute*
[2] *whose beauty is not naturally inherited, but comes instead from cosmetics*
[3] *seduced him, turned him against me*
[4] *no longer desirable*

The shock of reading Posthumus' letter leaves Imogen overwhelmed with pain and misery. In despair, she pulls Pisanio's sword from its sheath and offers it to him. She has no reason to go on living:

Imogen: Take it, and hit
The innocent mansion of my love, my heart.
Fear not, 'tis empty of all things but grief.
Thy master is not there, who was indeed
The riches of it.[1] Do his bidding, strike.

[1] *Posthumus' love for me, which was the treasure of my heart, is no longer there*

Pisanio takes the sword and throws it down. Imogen persists; to take her own life would be a mortal sin, so Pisanio must carry out Posthumus' command. She will offer no resistance, she promises. She indicates her heart, and as she does so she discovers earlier letters from her husband. They were loving and tender, and she had kept them close; now she scatters them forlornly to the ground.

Ready to die, Imogen addresses her husband as if for the last time. She reminds him that, in marrying him, she had to face the disapproval of her own father, the king. He will regret losing the love of a princess for the sake of a brief affair with his Roman lover, she warns him. She then orders Pisanio, once again, to kill her.

The situation is agonising for him too, Pisanio complains, but Imogen dismisses his concerns bluntly. His agony will be over as soon as his task is done:

Imogen: Prithee dispatch.[1]
The lamb entreats the butcher. Where's thy knife?
Thou art too slow to do thy master's bidding
When I desire it too.
Pisanio: O gracious lady,
Since I received command to do this business,
I have not slept one wink.
Imogen: Do't, and to bed then.

[1] *please do it quickly*

Pisanio continues to refuse; it is unthinkable that he should kill Imogen. Impatient and angry, she demands to know why he has gone to all the trouble of taking her on this long journey, with all its difficulties and dangers, if he did not intend to carry out Posthumus' command. Pisanio replies that the journey has provided him with time to think about Posthumus' letter; and he has come up with a plan that, with luck, might produce a happy outcome.

For centuries *Cymbeline* has divided opinion, probably more than any other Shakespeare play. The play's inconsistency and patent lack of realism tends to concern modern critics less than those of the past:

"To remark the folly of the fiction, the absurdity of the conduct, the confusion of the names and manners of different times, and the impossibility of the events in any system of life, were to waste criticism upon unresisting imbecility ..."

Samuel Johnson, *The Plays of William Shakespeare*, 1765

"It is for the most part stagey trash of the lowest melodramatic order, in parts abominably written, throughout intellectually vulgar, and judged in point of thought by modern intellectual standards, vulgar, foolish, offensive, indecent, and exasperating beyond all tolerance."

George Bernard Shaw, *Blaming the Bard*, 1896

"Cymbeline *is an astonishing piece of work, in the most literal sense ... in none of his other plays is there so much experimental daring as in* Cymbeline. *It is his most avant-garde work."*

John Wain, *The Living World of Shakespeare*, 1964

"Modern popular and critical audiences often prefer genre-crossing works like Cymbeline *... For a period such as ours that celebrates experimental form, ambiguity, intertextuality, and, above all, sensational drama,* Cymbeline *offers rich territory for exploration."*

Jennifer Forsyth, Introduction to *Cymbeline* in *Internet Shakespeare Editions*, 2020

A new identity

Imogen is ready to listen. Pisanio states, first, that she and her husband are clearly the victims of a terrible deception. Imogen, by contrast, is unable to shake off the thought that Posthumus has rejected her in favour of another woman:

Pisanio: It cannot be[1]
But that my master is abused.[2] Some villain,
Ay, and singular in his art,[3] hath done you both
This cursed injury.
Imogen: Some Roman courtesan.
Pisanio: No, on my life.

[1] *there can be no other explanation*
[2] *deceived, misled*
[3] *of unrivalled skill*

Pisanio continues. To keep Posthumus' trust, he will tell his master that he has killed Imogen as instructed, and will send a bloodstained garment of hers as proof. There is no question of Imogen's return to court, and even remaining in Britain is dangerous:

Imogen: No court, no father, nor no more ado
With that harsh, noble, simple nothing,
That Cloten, whose love-suit hath been to me
As fearful as a siege.
Pisanio: If not at court,
Then not in Britain must you bide.[1]

[1] *stay, live*

Pisanio explains that the Roman ambassador, Caius Lucius, is at Cymbeline's court. He will shortly be travelling to Milford Haven, where he will embark on his voyage back to Italy. If Imogen can find a way of joining the ambassador on his journey to Rome, she will be able to investigate her husband's activity more closely; with luck, she will discover the truth behind Posthumus' sudden, bewildering change of heart.

Imogen listens with growing enthusiasm. Her best course, continues Pisanio, is to ask Lucius to employ her as a servant. In order to do this, she must forget that she is a princess, and lose her air of calm authority; more drastically, she must disguise herself as a young man. Pisanio summarises the mannerisms she should adopt if she is to be convincing as a lively, self-confident youth:

Pisanio: … a waggish[1] courage,
Ready in gibes,[2] quick-answered, saucy, and
As quarrelous[3] as the weasel.

[1] *mischievous*
[2] *always ready to jeer and make sarcastic remarks*
[3] *quarrelsome; weasels were believed to be aggressive and short-tempered*

As well as putting on a display of brash self-assurance, Imogen must be prepared to work outdoors, under the sun, and will have to dispense with her usual fine clothes. It will not be easy, Pisanio warns her anxiously. Imogen, already warming to the idea, impatiently brushes aside his concerns:

Pisanio: Nay, you must
Forget that rarest treasure of your cheek,[1]
Exposing it – but O, the harder heart!
Alack, no remedy[2] – to the greedy touch
Of common-kissing Titan,[3] and forget
Your laboursome and dainty trims[4] …
Imogen: Nay, be brief.
I see into thy end[5] and am almost
A man already.

[1] *neglect your beautiful complexion*
[2] *it's unfortunate, but there's no alternative*
[3] *the sun god, who shines indiscriminately on everyone*
[4] *elaborate, ornate clothes*
[5] *I understand the point you're making*

Pisanio has brought suitable clothes for Imogen's transformation, and he now hands them over. He is confident that the princess, once disguised as a young man, will find employment with Lucius. Imogen too is now in good spirits, and is ready to set off to Milford Haven: once there, she will join the ambassador on the voyage to Rome, where she can at least be close to her beloved.

Pisanio must return to court as soon as possible. Imogen's absence will have been noticed by now; if it is discovered that her loyal servant is also missing, he will be suspected of involvement in her disappearance.

Just before the two of them go their separate ways, Pisanio remembers the box, given to him by the queen, that contains a restorative drug: having accidentally dropped it while he was in her presence, she had allowed him to keep it. Thinking that Imogen may well need a remedy of some kind on her long journey, Pisanio hands her the box:

Pisanio: My noble mistress,
Here is a box – I had it from the queen –
What's in't is precious. If you are sick at sea,
Or stomach-qualmed[1] at land, a dram of this
Will drive away distemper.[2]

[1] *queasy, nauseous*
[2] *illness*

Towards the end of his career, Shakespeare wrote a number of plays, like *Cymbeline*, that do not fit easily into the traditional categories of history, comedy or tragedy. One critic suggests that Shakespeare had simply lost interest in conventional forms:

"The plot is a chaos, and Shakespeare never bothers to be probable. Perhaps he was in a contrary mood and decided that this time he would please himself ... That is why its Rome is at once ancient and modern, and its Britain both Jacobean and archaic. Shakespeare had wearied of history, even as he had come to the end of both comedy and tragedy."

Harold Bloom, *Shakespeare: The Invention of the Human*, 1998

Missing

The ambassador Lucius has been recalled to Rome. He has been unable to persuade Cymbeline to pay the previously agreed tribute, and his visit to the British court is over. As he leaves he states, regretfully, that military action must follow. Cymbeline replies that Britain is bound to resist domination by the empire:

Cymbeline: Thus far, and so farewell.
Lucius: Thanks, royal sir.
My emperor hath wrote I must from hence,
And am right sorry that I must report ye
My master's enemy.
Cymbeline: Our subjects, sir,
Will not endure his yoke[1] …

[1] *control, oppression*

Despite the talk of war, the ambassador's personal relationship with Cymbeline is one of friendship and respect. Lucius is amiable and diplomatic even with the belligerent Cloten:

Lucius: Your hand, my lord.
Cloten: Receive it friendly, but from this time forth
I wear it as your enemy.
Lucius: Sir, the event
Is yet to name the winner.[1]

[1] *the winner will not be known until the conflict is over*

The king assures Lucius that he will be conducted in safety to Milford Haven, where he will board his ship for Rome.

When the ambassador has left, Cymbeline discusses the situation with the queen. An invasion is clearly imminent: however, the king has been aware of Rome's intentions for some time, particularly as Roman troops have been gathering in large numbers in France. Cymbeline is confident that effective preparations have been made, and that British cavalry and chariots will offer fierce resistance to the invaders.

War with Rome is not the king's only concern, however. Another matter is troubling him:

Cymbeline: … Where is our daughter? She hath not appeared
Before the Roman,[1] nor to us hath tendered
The duty of the day.[2] She looks us[3] like
A thing more made of malice than of duty;
We have noted it. Call her before us, for
We have been too slight in sufferance.[4]

[1] *to meet the ambassador from Rome*
[2] *nor has she given me her customary morning greeting, as is her duty*
[3] *appears to me*
[4] *too lenient in tolerating her behaviour*

A messenger immediately hurries away to find the princess. The queen asks her husband not to be too harsh on his daughter. Since Posthumus' banishment, the princess has become quiet and reclusive, and it will take time for her to recover:

Queen: Royal sir,
Since the exile of Posthumus, most retired[1]
Hath her life been, the cure whereof, my lord,
'Tis time must do. Beseech your majesty,
Forbear[2] sharp speeches to her.

[1] *withdrawn, solitary*
[2] *avoid, refrain from*

The messenger now returns. There is no sign of the princess: her door is locked, and despite continual knocking and calling there is no response from within her chamber. The queen assures Cymbeline that there is nothing to worry about; earlier, Imogen had specifically told her that she was unwell, and would spend the day in her room. Her words provide no comfort to the king, who rushes out in a state of agitation, fearing for his daughter's life:

Cymbeline: Her doors locked?
Not seen of late? Grant, heavens, that which I
Fear prove false.[1]

[1] *let my fears prove to be unfounded*

Cloten accompanies the king to find out what has happened to Imogen. As he leaves, he remarks that he has not seen her attendant Pisanio recently.

Now alone, the queen reveals her true feelings. As a loyal servant to both Posthumus and Imogen, Pisanio poses a threat to her. If he is missing, it may be because he has taken the drug she gave him, believing it to be an effective remedy; if so, he should be dead by now. As for Imogen, she may have taken her own life, or she may have run away to be with Posthumus. Either result will suit her purpose, as her own son can then inherit the throne of Britain:

Queen: Haply despair hath seized her,[1]
Or, winged with fervour of her love,[2] she's flown
To her desired Posthumus. Gone she is
To death or to dishonour, and my end[3]
Can make good use of either. She being down,
I have the placing of the British crown.[4]

[1] *perhaps her misery has led to her death*
[2] *driven on swiftly by the strength of her love*
[3] *aim, purpose*
[4] *the power to decide who will succeed to the throne*

Evil intentions

Cloten returns with news that the princess is nowhere to be found. Cymbeline, he reports, is in such a fit of fury that his courtiers dare not approach him. He asks the queen to see if she can calm him down. As she leaves, her whispered remark suggests that she hopes his overwhelming anger may prove fatal:

Cloten: Go in and cheer the king. He rages, none
Dare come about him.
Queen: [*aside*] All the better. May
This night forestall him of the coming day.[1]

[1] *prevent him from seeing another day*

Cloten broods on his feelings for Imogen. She is noble, admirable, and beautiful; he cannot deny that she is superior, in every respect, to any other woman he has known. However, she is utterly degraded, in his eyes, by her love for Posthumus. She must be punished for this dreadful mistake:

Cloten: … Disdaining me and throwing favours on
The low Posthumus slanders so her judgement
That what's else rare is choked,[1] and in that point
I will conclude to hate her, nay, indeed,
To be revenged upon her.

[1] *shows her judgement to be so untrustworthy that her otherwise exceptional qualities are stifled*

Pisanio now enters, and Cloten confronts him aggressively, demanding to know where Imogen has gone. Pisanio tries to avoid the question, but Cloten becomes increasingly forceful, eventually threatening him with death if he does not give a clear answer.

Pisanio reluctantly hands over the letter that Imogen had earlier discarded; it was from Posthumus, urging her to join him in Milford Haven. Although the letter gives away Imogen's whereabouts, Pisanio is confident that Cloten will not have time to catch up with her. If everything has gone according to plan, she will soon be leaving for Rome, as servant to Caius Lucius.

When Cloten has read the letter, his tone changes abruptly. His threatening manner vanishes, and instead he promises to reward Pisanio generously if he accepts the offer of a job. Cloten needs a servant; the man he is looking for must be reliable and honest, and at the same time prepared to undertake any task, however wicked and immoral. Cloten struggles to express his contradictory requirements:

Cloten: … if thou wouldst not be a villain but do me true service, undergo those employments wherein I should have cause to use thee with a serious industry[1] – that is, what villainy soe'er I bid thee do,[2] to perform it directly and truly – I would think thee an honest man.

[1] *carry out the tasks I give you carefully and diligently*
[2] *whatever wrongdoing I order you to commit*

Given that Pisanio has served the impoverished Posthumus in the past, he must surely be grateful for the opportunity to work for a rich, influential master, argues Cloten, such as himself. The two men shake hands, and Cloten gives Pisanio his first instruction:

Cloten:	Hast any of thy late[1] master's garments in thy possession?
Pisanio:	I have, my lord, at my lodging the same suit he wore when he took leave of my lady and mistress.
Cloten:	The first service thou dost me, fetch that suit hither.

[1] *previous*

Pisanio leaves to fetch Posthumus' clothes. Cloten then reveals the horrifying plan he has in mind. He still remembers Imogen's dismissive comment: she had more respect for Posthumus' meanest garment, she declared, than for Cloten. In revenge, he intends to travel to Milford Haven, hunt down the couple, kill Posthumus, and rape Imogen while wearing her husband's clothes. She will never again mock his character, his appearance, or his courage:

Cloten:	She said upon a time[1] ... that she held the very garment of Posthumus in more respect than my noble and natural person, together with the adornment of my qualities.[2] With that suit upon my back will I ravish[3] her – first kill him, and in her eyes.[4] There she shall see my valour ... She hath despised me rejoicingly, and I'll be merry in my revenge.

[1] *once*
[2] *both my innately noble appearance and the personal talents that enhance it*
[3] *rape*
[4] *in her sight, in front of her*

Pisanio now returns with Posthumus' clothes. He tells Cloten, encouragingly, that Imogen cannot have travelled far; in truth, he knows that she must be in or near Milford Haven by now, and about to depart to safety. With a warning to Pisanio to remain loyal, and to reveal nothing about his new master's intentions, Cloten sets off.

Alone, Pisanio can finally express the scorn and revulsion he feels for Cloten. He calls on the heavens to ensure that Imogen is safe:

Pisanio: To Milford go,
And find not her whom thou pursuest. Flow, flow,
You heavenly blessings on her. This fool's speed
Be crossed with slowness; labour be his meed.[1]

[1] *may Cloten's progress be hindered by delays, and may further difficulties be his only reward*

Lost

III, vi

Imogen has successfully disguised herself as a pageboy. She is ready to meet Lucius, the ambassador, and join him as his servant on the voyage to Rome. However, the final stage of her journey to Milford Haven is not proving as straightforward as she had hoped. Despite Pisanio's directions, she has been unable to find the town, and has been trudging wearily through the wilderness for the last two days:

Imogen: I see a man's life is a tedious one.
I have tired myself, and for two nights together
Have made the ground my bed. I should be sick
But that my resolution helps me.[1] Milford,
When from the mountain top Pisanio showed thee,
Thou wast within a ken.[2]

[1] *if it were not for the fact that I am so determined*
[2] *within sight, clearly visible*

As she wanders across the rugged mountainside, Imogen suddenly notices a path leading to the mouth of a cave. She is apprehensive about approaching but, driven on by hunger, she plucks up her courage and calls out. There is no answer, and she cautiously enters the cave.

Imogen draws her sword, hoping that, if she is faced with an opponent, he will be as terrified as she is:

Imogen: Ho! No answer? Then I'll enter.
Best draw my sword, and if mine enemy
But fear the sword like me, he'll scarcely look on't.[1]
Such a foe, good heavens.[2]

[1] *he'll hardly have the courage to look at it*
[2] *may the heavens grant me a foe as fearful as I am*

An unexpected guest

Belarius and the two boys, returning from the hunt, now approach their cave. They have been successful; Guiderius, the older brother, has killed an animal, and the other two, as is their tradition, will cook and serve. Belarius goes inside, but almost immediately hurries out again, warning the boys not to enter. There is a strange, beautiful creature in their home, a boy who seems almost too delicate and flawless to be human:

Belarius: Stay, come not in.
But that it eats our victuals,[1] I should think
Here were a fairy.
Guiderius: What's the matter, sir?
Belarius: By Jupiter, an angel – or if not,
An earthly paragon.[2]

[1] *if it weren't eating our food*
[2] *a perfect specimen, as close to an angel as can be found on earth*

Imogen now emerges from the cave, apologising profusely and begging to be treated mercifully. She only entered because she was desperate with hunger, she explains, and fully intends to pay for the food that she has taken. The young men are amused at the mention of money; out in this remote place, silver and gold mean nothing to them.

In her guise as a pageboy, Imogen has chosen the name Fidele. She explains that she is on her way to Milford Haven, where she is to embark on her voyage to Italy. Belarius welcomes the young stranger warmly, inviting him to stay and dine with them:

Belarius: Prithee, fair youth,
Think us no churls,[1] nor measure our good minds
By this rude[2] place we live in. Well encountered.
'Tis almost night; you shall have better cheer[3]
Ere you depart, and thanks[4] to stay and eat it.

[1] *mean-spirited peasants*
[2] *rustic, unsophisticated*
[3] *food, hospitality*
[4] *we will thank you*

The two young men are delighted with their new friend, and declare that he is as welcome as if he were their brother. For a moment Imogen wishes, secretly, that they really were her brothers; she would not then be heiress to the throne, and her marriage to Posthumus would not have caused such turmoil in her life.

It is time to prepare their evening feast, announces Belarius. Keen to learn more about their new acquaintance Fidele, he urges them all to enter the cave.

> *"... against the miasma of Italian gentility and the cruder corruption of the British court Shakespeare has put the mountain atmosphere of Wales. These scenes are among the loveliest in Shakespeare. They are done with a gusto that shows how deeply the poet's heart was in them. We feel ourselves bounding up the rocks, leaping the brooks, drinking in the bracing air ... The mountains of Wales in this play are all that Italy and the British court are not."*
>
> Harold C. Goddard, *The Meaning of Shakespeare*, 1951

Preparing for victory

III, vii

In Rome, a senator delivers an important message, direct from the emperor, to a senior military officer. The Roman Empire is already fighting on a number of fronts, and the invasion of Britain will stretch the army even further. Accordingly, the emperor has decreed that the existing troops must be supplemented by civilians drawn from the ranks of the gentry.

The officer has full authority, the senator informs him, to enlist the necessary combatants from the Roman nobility. Those ordered to join the invasion have no choice but to accept their commission.

The senator also mentions that Caius Lucius, who has served as ambassador to Britain, will not be returning to Rome as planned: instead, he will take command of the Roman troops once they arrive at the port of Milford Haven. Following the invasion – which, it is assumed, will be successful – Lucius will become governor of the Roman province of Britain.

Malice aforethought

IV, i

Another figure is wandering through the rugged, inhospitable wilderness outside Milford Haven: this time it is Cloten, the queen's son. According to the letter that Pisanio showed him, Posthumus and his wife should be in the vicinity; in the letter, Posthumus stated that he had secretly returned from exile, and asked Imogen to come and meet him.

Cloten is wearing Posthumus' clothes. The fact that they fit him so well prompts the thought that Imogen should find him just as appealing as her husband:

Cloten: How fit his garments serve me![1] Why should his mistress, who was made by him that made the tailor,[2] not be fit[3] too?

[1] *how perfectly his clothes suit me*
[2] *who was made by the same God as everyone else; who is only human*
[3] *a good match for me, attracted to me*

Continuing with his line of thought, Cloten compares himself to his rival. He decides that he is Posthumus' equal or superior in every respect, although some of his claims are dubious:

Cloten: … the lines of my body are as well drawn as his: no less young, more strong, not beneath him in fortunes, beyond him in the advantage of the time,[1] above him in birth, alike conversant in general services,[2] and more remarkable in single oppositions.[3]

[1] *currently in more favourable circumstances*
[2] *equally experienced in military matters*
[3] *individual fights at close quarters*

It is a mystery to Cloten why the princess has chosen Posthumus instead of him. However, he intends to remedy the situation in the most violent way possible:

Cloten: Posthumus, thy head, which now is growing upon thy shoulders, shall within this hour be off, thy mistress enforced,[1] thy garments cut to pieces before her face …

[1] *assaulted, raped*

By raping Imogen while wearing her husband's clothes, Cloten will, in his mind, be inflicting the punishment she deserves for her earlier rejection of his advances. With Posthumus dead, Cloten will return to court with the princess. The king will no doubt be shocked, he reasons, but the queen is sure to take his side:

Cloten: … all this done, spurn[1] her home to her father, who may haply[2] be a little angry for my so rough usage; but my mother, having power of his testiness,[3] shall turn all into my commendations.[4]

[1] *I'll kick*
[2] *perhaps*
[3] *the ability to deal with his short temper*
[4] *make sure that I emerge from the episode with credit*

Impatient for revenge, Cloten draws his sword and sets off in search of his victims.

Fidele takes to his bed

IV, ii

It is morning, and Belarius is outside the cave with his two boys. Imogen, in her guise as the young pageboy Fidele, is with them. Her arduous journey through the wilderness has taken its toll, however, and she has fallen ill.

Guiderius and Arviragus are concerned; they have grown very fond of Fidele, and think of him almost as a brother. Guiderius offers to stay with him while the other two set out on their morning hunt, but Fidele insists that he would rather be on his own. The two youths, moved by their compassion for the sick boy, declare their feelings for him. They cannot deny that they feel as close to Fidele as to their own father:

Guiderius: [*to Fidele*] I love thee: I have spoke it,
How much the quantity, the weight as much,[1]
As I do love my father.
Belarius: What? How, how?
Arviragus: If it be sin to say so, sir, I yoke me
In my good brother's fault.[2] I know not why
I love this youth, and I have heard you say,
Love's reason's without reason.[3]

[1] *as much, and as intensely*
[2] *I am just as guilty as my brother*
[3] *love is not guided by logic*

Belarius does not resent the boys' declarations. Unlike them, he is aware that he is not their true father, and he admires their innate nobility in speaking their minds so freely.

As the three men prepare for the hunt, Imogen remarks to herself that the view of rustic life widely held at court is nothing like the reality:

Imogen: [*aside*] These are kind creatures. Gods, what lies I have heard.
Our courtiers say all's savage but[1] at court.
Experience, O thou disprov'st report!

[1] *except*

Feeling unwell, and still weighed down with her worries about Posthumus, Imogen remembers the medicine that Pisanio gave her earlier, recommending it as an effective universal remedy. She finds the box he gave her, opens it, and swallows the drug. Taking her leave, she goes back into the cave to lie down.

The others, fascinated by their guest, cannot resist speculating about his origins and why he has come to this remote spot. Fidele has told them that he is of noble birth, but has fallen on hard times. They know no more than that, but are intrigued by his talents. He is even an accomplished cook, as they discovered when he helped to prepare dinner yesterday:

Belarius: This youth, howe'er distressed,[1] appears he hath had
Good ancestors.
Arviragus: How angel-like he sings!
Guiderius: But his neat[2] cookery! He cut our roots in characters[3] ...

[1] *impoverished, unfortunate*
[2] *dainty*
[3] *shapes and letters*

Guiderius and Arviragus agree, however, that something is clearly troubling the youth; he seems to be burdened by some unspoken sadness that he can never completely hide. Their thoughts are interrupted as Belarius points out that it is broad daylight, and time to set off into the mountains.

Picking a fight

Just as they are about to leave, Belarius suddenly becomes aware that there is a stranger nearby. It is Cloten, sword at the ready, stumbling furiously through the rough terrain. He curses Pisanio, who seems to have directed him to the wrong place. Posthumus and Imogen are nowhere to be found:

Cloten: I cannot find those runagates;[1] that villain
Hath mocked me.[2] I am faint.

[1] *runaways, fugitives*
[2] *tricked me, made a fool of me*

Belarius, overhearing the angry outburst, is shocked and dismayed. He has lived in his mountain hideaway, undiscovered, for nearly twenty years; but now, it seems, the authorities have finally caught up with him. He recognises the man as the queen's son, and the runaways he is searching for are clearly Belarius himself and the two boys.

Belarius tells the boys to flee, but Guiderius has a different idea. He will confront the attacker himself, while Belarius and Arviragus quickly search the surrounding countryside to check whether Cloten has brought any followers with him.

Cloten notices the two figures running off, and then encounters Guiderius. Remote areas like these are notorious for harbouring criminals, Cloten believes, and he assumes that he has come across a group of bandits. He challenges the youth to surrender:

Cloten: Soft,[1] what are you
That fly me thus? Some villain mountaineers?[2]
I have heard of such. What slave[3] art thou?
Guiderius: A thing
More slavish did I ne'er than answering
A slave without a knock.[4]
Cloten: Thou art a robber,
A law-breaker, a villain. Yield thee, thief.

[1] *wait, stop*
[2] *mountain dwellers*
[3] *delinquent, low life*
[4] *I have never done anything more disreputable than respond to an insulting rogue without hitting him*

Guiderius is scornful of the aggressive, loud-mouthed stranger. Unwilling to fight such a foolish adversary, he asks Cloten to leave him alone. Cloten, with increasing frustration, attempts to intimidate his opponent by revealing his noble background. Guiderius remains unmoved:

Cloten: Thou injurious thief,
Hear but my name and tremble.
Guiderius: What's thy name?
Cloten: Cloten, thou villain.
Guiderius: Cloten, thou double villain be thy name,
I cannot tremble at it …

Finally Cloten triumphantly announces the one fact that will, he is certain, terrify the youth into submission:

Cloten: To thy further fear,
Nay, to thy mere confusion,[1] thou shalt know
I am son to th' queen.
Guiderius: I am sorry for't, not seeming[2]
So worthy as thy birth.
Cloten: Art not afeard?
Guiderius: Those that I reverence, those I fear,[3] the wise.
At fools I laugh, not fear them.

[1] *utter devastation*
[2] *since you do not seem*
[3] *those are the people I regard with awe*

Cloten can no longer tolerate the boy's insolence. He will be executed for his lack of respect; after that, Cloten will hunt down the other two, who will be punished in the same way. The heads of the three criminals will be taken back to London for public display. Sword in hand, Cloten approaches Guiderius and begins to lash out.

> *"Unlike verbal Posthumus, physical Cloten and devious Iachimo, Guiderius and Arviragus combine physical competence in hunting with ritual observance, brotherly collaboration and respectful resistance to paternal authority. They know when to fight and when to mourn, in contrast to the three men bent on violence, war and seduction. In a play that stages repeated male contests, Guiderius and Arviragus are the only consistent winners ..."*
>
> Valerie Wayne, Introduction to the Arden Shakespeare edition of *Cymbeline*, 2017

An unlamented death

Belarius and Arviragus return, having explored the surrounding area for any companions who might be helping Cloten in his search. They have found no one, and Arviragus wonders whether the lone intruder really was the queen's son. Belarius is sure, despite the passage of so many years, that he recognised Cloten from his own time at court. He is concerned for Guiderius' safety as even then, he recalls, Cloten was a dangerous, unpredictable individual.

Belarius is rendered almost speechless as Guiderius returns: he is carrying Cloten's severed head. The young man calmly dismisses his father's concerns. Cloten's belligerent, insulting manner was bad enough, Guiderius explains; more importantly, however, the intruder had intended to kill them all. Whatever his social status, the man had to be stopped:

Belarius: What hast thou done?
Guiderius: I am perfect what:[1] cut off one Cloten's head,
Son to the queen, after his own report,[2]
Who called me traitor, mountaineer, and swore
With his own single hand he'd take us in,[3]
Displace our heads where, thank the gods, they grow,
And set them on Lud's town.[4]
Belarius: We are all undone.

[1] *I am perfectly aware of what I have done*
[2] *according to him*
[3] *overcome us*
[4] *display our heads in London*

Cloten, despite his reckless, impetuous nature, has surely not come to track them down on his own, Belarius feels. He is convinced that there must be other courtiers close behind, determined to find the three of them. Although he appreciates the courage shown by Guiderius, he is fearful of the revenge that will surely follow.

Belarius is aware that he committed a serious crime when he abducted the king's two boys from court all those years ago. The boys themselves, by contrast, know nothing of their early years, and are unafraid of the consequences of Cloten's death. Guiderius remarks contemptuously that he intends to dispose of the severed head in the sea:

Guiderius: With his own sword,
Which he did wave against my throat, I have ta'en
His head from him. I'll throw't into the creek
Behind our rock,[1] and let it to the sea[2]
And tell the fishes he's the queen's son, Cloten.
That's all I reck.[3]

Belarius: I fear 'twill be revenged.
Would, Polydore, thou hadst not done't, though valour
Becomes[4] thee well enough.

1 *cave*
2 *let it float out to sea*
3 *that's how much I care about his death*
4 *suits*

As Guiderius leaves, his younger brother expresses the wish that he had had the opportunity to kill their attacker. If revenge follows, he will be only too happy to face it:

Arviragus: Would I had done't,
So the revenge alone pursued me.[1] Polydore,
I love thee brotherly, but envy much
Thou hast robbed me of this deed.

1 *I wish that I had killed Cloten, and that I could face the ensuing reprisals on my own*

Belarius calls off the day's hunting; the events of the morning have left him weary and shaken. Besides, he is anxious about young Fidele, who woke in a fragile state of health, and has been resting in the cave all morning. He sends Arviragus to join their young guest while he waits outside for Guiderius to return.

Now alone, Belarius reflects again on the natural nobility that the two boys seem to possess despite their unsophisticated, secluded upbringing:

Belarius: They are as gentle
As zephyrs blowing below the violet,
Not wagging his sweet head,[1] and yet as rough,
Their royal blood enchafed,[2] as the rud'st wind
That by the top doth take[3] the mountain pine
And make him stoop to th' vale.[4]

[1] *mild breezes that blow softly through the violets without disturbing the flower heads*
[2] *aroused, angered*
[3] *seize, uproot*
[4] *fall to the valley floor*

Their good qualities seem to have developed without the benefit of formal education, and without the presence of courtiers or others who might set an example:

Belarius: 'Tis wonder
That an invisible instinct should frame[1] them
To royalty unlearned, honour untaught,
Civility not seen from other,[2] valour
That wildly grows in them but yields a crop
As if it had been sowed.[3]

[1] *guide, instruct*
[2] *courtesy not imitated from other people*
[3] *courage that grows naturally in them, but develops as if it had been specially cultivated*

Guiderius returns, having discarded Cloten's head in the nearby creek. He and Belarius are about to go inside when they are stopped in their tracks: strange, solemn music suddenly fills the air, and it is coming from inside their cave.

An untimely end

The instrument producing the mournful sound belongs to Belarius. It has not been used since the death of Euriphile, the boys' nurse, always believed by Guiderius and Arviragus to be their mother.

At first, Guiderius is indignant that his brother should be playing the instrument without good reason. As the sound dies down and Arviragus emerges from the cave, however, it becomes clear why he has been playing such sorrowful music. He is carrying Fidele's lifeless body in his arms:

Arviragus: The bird is dead
That we have made so much on.[1] I had rather
Have skipped from sixteen years of age to sixty,
To have turned my leaping time into a crutch,[2]
Than have seen this.

[1] *cherished, held dear*
[2] *given up the agility of youth for the frailty of age*

Belarius, like the two brothers, is stunned by Fidele's death. The mysterious sadness that he seemed to harbour, Belarius believes, finally proved too much for the boy:

Belarius: Thou blessed thing,
Jove knows what man thou mightst have made, but I,[1]
Thou diedst a most rare boy, of melancholy.

[1] *but all I know is that*

Arviragus addresses the dead boy lovingly, assuring him that his grave will be tended with care and devotion:

Arviragus: With fairest flowers
Whilst summer lasts and I live here, Fidele,
I'll sweeten thy sad grave. Thou shalt not lack
The flower that's like thy face, pale primrose, nor
The azured harebell,[1] like thy veins; no, nor
The leaf of eglantine[2] ...

[1] *bluebell*
[2] *delicately scented wild rose*

... The azured harebell, like thy veins ...

Cymbeline was probably written at a time when the London theatres were closed – as they so often were – due to a prolonged outbreak of the plague, with dozens of deaths every week in the capital.

It seems likely that Shakespeare, having lived mainly in London for the previous fifteen years, decided at this stage to spend more time in his home town of Stratford-upon-Avon. Avoiding the plague may have been one deciding factor; he had also, some years before, bought a large house with extensive grounds in Stratford. His wife and daughters were there, and he had also invested in land in the area.

Some critics feel that the move from the busy capital to a small rural market town, surrounded by forest and farmland, had a distinct influence on Shakespeare's writing:

"It is perhaps in Cymbeline *that Shakespeare's art of natural observation is at its most acute ... It is unlikely to be a coincidence that Shakespeare turned to pastoral romance in the plague years around 1607–10: of all his plays,* Cymbeline *and* The Winter's Tale *are the ones that have the most distinctive air of having been written back home in Stratford."*

Jonathan Bate, *Soul of the Age*, 2008

Uncomfortable with his brother's sentimentality, Guiderius interrupts, insisting that they must face the reality of what has happened:

Guiderius: Prithee have done,[1]
And do not play in wench-like[2] words with that
Which is so serious. Let us bury him
And not protract with admiration what
Is now due debt to th' grave.[3]

[1] *please stop*
[2] *girlish*
[3] *let us not delay, with our admiration for Fidele, the burial that is now necessary*

Fidele's body must be buried next to that of their mother, they decide. The funeral rites, too, should be just as they were for Euriphile, although the brothers no longer have the sweet voices of their childhood:

Arviragus: Say, where shall's lay him?
Guiderius: By good Euriphile, our mother.
Arviragus: Be't so,[1]
And let us, Polydore, though now our voices
Have got the mannish crack,[2] sing him to th' ground
As once to our mother …

[1] *let it be so*
[2] *have broken*

Guiderius' singing voice is not good enough, he confesses, to do justice to the occasion, so the boys decide to recite Fidele's funeral song instead. Belarius now mentions Cloten. He too must be given a suitable burial, despite his cruel intentions:

Belarius: He was a queen's son, boys,
And though he came our enemy, remember
He was paid[1] for that.
… Our foe was princely,
And though you took his life as being our foe,
Yet bury him as a prince.

[1] *punished*

Belarius leaves to fetch Cloten's headless corpse.

Farewell

The brothers carefully lay Fidele out in a suitable spot. Tradition dictates that the body must be correctly aligned:

Guiderius: Nay, Cadwal, we must lay his head to th' east.
My father hath a reason for't.
Arviragus: 'Tis true.

The older of the two begins the recital. The funeral song, addressed to Fidele, reassures him that the worries of everyday life are now over. Like flowers that must eventually go to seed and die, humanity shares a common fate:

Fear no more the heat o'th' sun,
Nor the furious winter's rages,
Thou thy worldly task hast done,
Home art gone and ta'en thy wages.
Golden lads and girls all must,
As chimney-sweepers,[1] come to dust.

[1] *the seed heads of dandelions, resembling chimney sweeps' brushes*

Golden lads and girls all must,
As chimney-sweepers, come to dust.

"One of the most beautiful lyrics in Shakespeare is the funeral dirge for Fidele in Cymbeline. *This lyric lists items in the natural and political worlds that must fade and die ... 'Chimney-sweepers', with its Victorian associations, seems a curiously inept image in the elegy; for a long time it perplexed editors. It was not until the twentieth century that researchers discovered that 'chimney-sweeper' is Warwickshire dialect for dandelion, the weed whose mature flower (which resembles the chimney-sweeper's brush) is a suitably fragile and evanescent symbol for this poem about transience."*

Laurie Maguire and Emma Smith, *30 Great Myths about Shakespeare*, 2013

Arviragus speaks the next verse. The song continues with its theme of comfort and inevitability; no one can harm Fidele now. The lives of the wise, the rich and the powerful will all take the same course as his:

Fear no more the frown o'th' great,
  Thou art past[1] the tyrant's stroke.
Care no more to clothe and eat,
  To thee the reed is as the oak.[2]
The sceptre, learning, physic must
All follow this[3] and come to dust.

[1] *beyond, out of reach*
[2] *there is no distinction between weakness and strength*
[3] *kings, scholars and doctors must all follow this path*

The two brothers share the final verses. There will be no more threats to Fidele from the natural world, and people with malicious motives can no longer harm him. His peace will be undisturbed by emotions of any kind:

Fear no more the lightning flash,
  Nor th'all-dreaded thunder-stone.[1]
Fear not slander, censure rash,[2]
  Thou hast finished joy and moan.[3]
All lovers young, all lovers must
Consign to thee[4] and come to dust.

[1] *thunderbolt, lightning strike*
[2] *harsh condemnation*
[3] *both happiness and sadness*
[4] *accept the same fate as you*

While Fidele's safety from earthly dangers is assured, the brothers pray that he will equally be protected from evil spirits:

No exorcizer[1] harm thee,
  Nor no witchcraft charm thee.
Ghost unlaid forbear thee.[2]
  Nothing ill come near thee.
Quiet consummation[3] have,
And renowned be thy grave.

[1] *one who can summon the spirits of the dead*
[2] *may you not be disturbed by any ghost that has not been laid to rest*
[3] *fulfilment, completion of your life*

Belarius now returns with Cloten's corpse. He lays it next to Fidele, and scatters flowers and herbs over the two bodies. Then, sadly and respectfully, Belarius and the two boys withdraw from the scene.

Awakening

The drug that Imogen had taken was not, as she believed, a restorative medicine. Pisanio had given it to her in good faith; but he had been tricked into accepting it by the queen, who believed it was a lethal poison. However, the queen too had been tricked by her physician, Cornelius. Suspicious of the queen's demand for poison, he had instead supplied her with a powerful sedative that would provoke a sleep so deep that it resembled death.

Fortunately the doctor was skilful in his preparation of the drug. It has had its intended effect, and Imogen now awakes from her long slumber. Drowsy and confused, she imagines she is still in mid-conversation, asking for directions to the port:

Imogen: Yes, sir, to Milford Haven, which is the way?
I thank you. By yond bush? Pray, how far thither?
'Od's pittikins:[1] can it be six mile yet?
I have gone all night.

[1] *Lord have mercy*

The journey has been long and tortuous and, in her muddled state, Imogen decides to lie down and rest. She recoils in shock as she realises that there is a man's body next to her. It is covered in flowers, but under them blood is distinctly visible. Imogen is certain that she has already had one strange dream, and she hopes desperately that this is another:

Imogen: I hope I dream,
For so[1] I thought I was a cave-keeper[2]
And cook to honest creatures. But 'tis not so.
'Twas but a bolt of nothing, shot at nothing[3] …

[1] *in that state; while I was dreaming*
[2] *cave dweller*
[3] *it didn't happen; it was like an arrow made of nothing, shot into nowhere*

It soon becomes clear to Imogen that she is not dreaming, and the body next to her is real and tangible. She then discovers, to her horror, that it has been decapitated; and she is utterly devastated when, looking more closely, she realises that the man is her husband Posthumus. She recognises his clothes, as well as his muscular form, which is almost godlike in her eyes:

Imogen: A headless man? The garments of Posthumus?
I know the shape of 's leg; this is his hand,
His foot Mercurial,[1] his Martial[2] thigh,
The brawns[3] of Hercules …

[1] *like that of Mercury, the fleet-footed messenger of the gods*
[2] *like that of Mars, the god of war*
[3] *muscles*

Horror and grief quickly give way to anger as Imogen realises who the perpetrators must be. Pisanio – probably bribed by Cloten – has undoubtedly carried out this dreadful crime. The letter instructing him to kill Imogen was clearly a forgery, designed to give Pisanio a reason to come to Milford Haven.

Pisanio's true motive had not been to accompany Imogen on her journey, she decides, but to murder Posthumus out here in the wilderness, far from any possible witnesses. The fact that he has tried to poison her confirms his guilt:

Imogen: Damned Pisanio
Hath with his forged letters – damned Pisanio –
From this most bravest vessel of the world
Struck the main-top! [1]
… 'Tis he and Cloten: malice and lucre in them
Have laid this woe here.[2] O, 'tis pregnant, pregnant! [3]
The drug he gave me, which he said was precious
And cordial to me, have I not found it
Murd'rous to th' senses? That confirms it home.[4]
This is Pisanio's deed, and Cloten.

[1] *cut off the top of the main mast; beheaded*
[2] *this tragic scene is the result of their envy and greed*
[3] *evident, clear*
[4] *beyond doubt*

Distraught, Imogen smears her face with the blood of her beloved, and clings tightly to his lifeless corpse.

Is Imogen's grief tragic or comic?

"When Imogen discovers what she believes to be her husband's beheaded corpse, her grief is so poignant and genuine that even while it often moves people in the audience to tears, they may simultaneously be snickering guiltily at the dramatic irony that the dead man is actually the malevolent Cloten, which adds a hefty dose of the ludicrous to Imogen's plight. Critics have tended to reduce the emotional significance to a single effect and thus have hailed it either as one of the most poignantly touching scenes ever written or as a scene so howlingly funny that it can only be a satire. Either *can be true, of course, partially depending on how it is played, but* both *can be true as well …"*

Jennifer Forsyth, Introduction to *Cymbeline* in *Internet Shakespeare Editions*, 2020

Rome on the move

The threatened Roman invasion of Britain is under way. Caius Lucius was originally sent to Britain as ambassador; however, now that negotiations have failed, he will not be returning to Rome, but has instead been ordered to take charge of the invading Roman troops.

A number of Roman legions have already made the journey from France and are now in Milford Haven, awaiting orders. Lucius, on his way to join them, is discussing the situation with an army captain. The troops already in Milford Haven will be reinforced, the captain reports, with men from the heart of the empire. They will be led by a renowned Roman nobleman:

Captain: The senate hath stirred up[1] the confiners[2]
And gentlemen of Italy, most willing spirits
That promise noble service, and they come
Under the conduct of bold Iachimo …

[1] *roused; recruited*
[2] *inhabitants; those living within the borders of Italy*

Lucius is pleased to hear that the additional Italian forces will be arriving shortly. He is confident that Rome will triumph in its conquest of Britain, and the soothsayer accompanying him strengthens his optimism. Last night, the soothsayer claims, he received a sign from the gods themselves:

Soothsayer: Last night the very gods showed me a vision –
I fast, and prayed for their intelligence[1] – thus:
I saw Jove's bird, the Roman eagle, winged
From the spongy south[2] to this part of the west,
There vanished in the sunbeams, which portends,
Unless my sins abuse my divination,[3]
Success to th' Roman host.[4]
Lucius: Dream often so,
And never false.

[1] *I fasted, and prayed for information*
[2] *flying from the damp, marshy south*
[3] *unless my sins have impaired my ability to communicate with the gods*
[4] *army*

A change of role

Lucius suddenly comes across a strange, gruesome sight: he notices a headless body on the ground, along with a young pageboy who appears to be resting on it. Whoever the corpse may have been in life, he was clearly a fine figure of a man:

Lucius: Soft,[1] ho, what trunk is here
Without his top? The ruin speaks[2] that sometime
It was a worthy building. How, a page?
Or[3] dead or sleeping on him?

[1] *wait a moment*
[2] *suggests, indicates*
[3] *either*

The pageboy must be dead too, Lucius assumes, believing that no one would choose to sleep on a corpse. However, an attendant confirms that the boy is alive. Lucius is intrigued, and wants to know more. Now that Posthumus is dead, however, Imogen has little to say:

Lucius: What's thy interest
In this sad wrack?[1] How came't? Who is't?
What art thou?
Imogen: I am nothing; or if not,
Nothing to be were better.[2] This was my master,
A very valiant Briton …

[1] *ruin; disfigured body*
[2] *whatever I may be, it would be better to be nothing*

Lucius, touched by the boy's plight, asks the name of his dead master. Unwilling to reveal Posthumus' true identity to the Romans, Imogen claims that he was killed by outlaws living in the mountains, and gives a false name:

Lucius: 'Lack,[1] good youth,
Thou mov'st no less with thy complaining than
Thy master in bleeding.[2] Say his name, good friend.
Imogen: Richard du Champ. [*aside*] If I do lie and do
No harm by it, though[3] the gods hear, I hope
They'll pardon it.

[1] *alas, what a pity*
[2] *your grief is just as moving as the sight of your dead master*
[3] *if*

Why 'Richard du Champ'?

Richard Field was a printer and bookseller. He was born, like Shakespeare, in Stratford-upon-Avon, and the two had been friends since childhood. As young men, both had moved to London to pursue their professions. It is very likely that they stayed in touch, as Field printed the first editions of Shakespeare's early poems.

Apart from Shakespeare's poetry, Field printed books and pamphlets in a variety of languages, including Latin, Spanish and French. He would often change his name to match the language of the publication; for example, he identified himself as 'Ricardo del Campo' on the title pages of his Spanish books.

In giving the name 'Richard du Champ' to the headless torso of the obnoxious Cloten, was Shakespeare enjoying a joke at his friend's expense?

When Lucius hears that the pageboy is named Fidele, meaning faithful, he remarks that the name clearly suits the boy as he has stayed so loyally with his dead master. Lucius has taken to the boy and, on a sudden impulse, offers to employ him as a servant:

Lucius: … Thy name well fits thy faith, thy faith thy name.
Wilt take thy chance with me? I will not say
Thou shalt be so well mastered,[1] but be sure
No less beloved.

[1] *I cannot promise to be the equal of your previous master*

Imogen agrees to serve Lucius, asking only for permission to bury her master first. Realising that Fidele only has his bare hands to dig a grave, Lucius hastily assembles a group of soldiers. He orders them to carry the body away and give it an honourable burial. As Cloten's headless corpse is borne away, Lucius tries to console his new servant:

Lucius: My friends,
The boy hath taught us manly duties. Let us
Find out the prettiest daisied plot we can,
And make him with our pikes and partisans[1]
A grave …
[*to Fidele*] Be cheerful, wipe thine eyes.
Some falls are means the happier to arise.[2]

[1] *spears and axes*
[2] *sometimes we can emerge from misfortunes happier than we were before*

Rising anxiety

IV, iii

Back in Cymbeline's court, things are going from bad to worse. Cloten has inexplicably gone missing, and his mother, the queen, is gravely ill with worry. Imogen too has disappeared, leaving the king bereft. Meanwhile, an invasion force from Rome is expected at any time:

Cymbeline: Heavens,
How deeply you at once do touch[1] me. Imogen,
The great part of my comfort, gone; my queen
Upon a desperate bed,[2] and in a time
When fearful wars point at me; her son gone,
So needful for this present.[3] It strikes me past
The hope of comfort.

[1] *afflict, distress*
[2] *desperately ill; on her deathbed*
[3] *who is indispensable in the present circumstances*

The king turns to Pisanio. A cloud of suspicion hangs over him; he was the princess's loyal servant, and must know something about her disappearance. Cymbeline threatens him with torture, but Pisanio pleads his innocence, and one of the king's attendants speaks up for him:

Cymbeline: … for thee, fellow,
Who needs must[1] know of her departure and
Dost seem so ignorant, we'll enforce it from thee
By a sharp torture.
Pisanio: Sir, my life is yours:
I humbly set it at your will. But for my mistress,
I nothing know where she remains, why gone,
Nor when she purposes[2] return. Beseech your highness,
Hold me your loyal servant.
Lord: Good my liege,
The day that she was missing, he[3] was here.
I dare be bound he's true[4] …

[1] *must surely*
[2] *intends to*
[3] *Pisanio*
[4] *swear he's telling the truth*

Cymbeline agrees, reluctantly, to let the matter rest for the present. He is then informed that troops of the Roman Empire, drawn both from France and from Rome itself, are now on British soil:

Lord: So please your majesty,
The Roman legions, all from Gallia[1] drawn,
Are landed on your coast with a supply
Of Roman gentlemen by the senate sent.
Cymbeline: Now for the counsel[2] of my son and queen!
I am amazed with matter.[3]

[1] *France*
[2] *if only I had the advice*
[3] *overwhelmed by events*

The king's attendants try to lift his spirits, assuring him that Britain is well prepared to resist the invaders. The British troops are ready and eager to fight, and all that is needed is for Cymbeline to issue his orders. The king leaves with his entourage; it is time to organise the country's response to the invasion.

Alone, Pisanio reveals his bewilderment at the current situation. He has not heard from his master Posthumus, nor from Imogen; even Cloten's whereabouts are a mystery.

In order to protect Imogen, Pisanio has hidden the truth about her flight to Milford Haven, but his loyalty to the king is as strong as ever. He intends to play his part in resisting the Roman invasion, even if he dies in the conflict. All his other concerns are in the hands of fate:

Pisanio: Wherein I am false, I am honest;[1] not true, to be true.
These present wars shall find I love my country
Even to the note o'th' king,[2] or I'll fall in them.
All other doubts, by time let them be cleared:
Fortune brings in some boats that are not steered.[3]

[1] *I have lied about my knowledge of Imogen, but for honest motives*
[2] *so much that the king himself will notice my valour*
[3] *sometimes fortune brings about a happy outcome without our intervention*

The onslaught begins

IV, iv

The Romans, having landed at Milford Haven, are now advancing. From outside their cave, Belarius and the young brothers can hear the confused, raucous sounds of war.

They must find a safe place away from the conflict, says Belarius. Arviragus disagrees; he is impatient to be in the thick of battle, fighting off the invaders. His older brother also disagrees, but for more practical reasons. If they attempt to hide their fate will be sealed, either immediately or at a later stage:

Arviragus: What pleasure, sir, find we in life, to lock it[1]
From action and adventure?
Guiderius: Nay, what hope
Have we in hiding us? This way[2] the Romans
Must or[3] for Britons slay us, or receive us
For barbarous and unnatural revolts
During their use,[4] and slay us after.

[1] *shut it off*
[2] *if we try to hide*
[3] *either*
[4] *forcibly enlist us as treacherous rebels, using us to fight against our own people until we are no longer needed*

Belarius insists that they should take refuge high in the mountains. If they join the British forces, he argues, they will be questioned about their identity and background. Sooner or later, the truth about Cloten's death will emerge, and they will be executed. The boys dismiss his reasoning; the army will be too concerned with the immediate threat posed by the invasion to bother with such questions.

Belarius reminds them that he was a well-known figure both at court and in military circles before his banishment, and might attract attention if he were to reappear. Besides, his banishment was entirely undeserved, based as it was on nothing more than a malicious rumour. He owes no loyalty to the king who so unjustly sent him into exile and forced him into a life of hardship.

Guiderius replies that these events belong to the distant past. He believes that all three of them should join the British ranks. No one will remember Belarius now; besides, his appearance has changed radically since his days at court. Arviragus, still excited at the prospect of battle, does not want to miss the opportunity. His only experience of conflict has been the hunting of wild animals:

Guiderius: Pray, sir, to th' army.[1]
I and my brother are not known; yourself
So out of thought, and thereto so o'ergrown,
Cannot be questioned.[2]
Arviragus: By this sun that shines
I'll thither.[3] What thing is't[4] that I never
Did see man die, scarce ever looked on blood
But that of coward hares …

[1] *let's join the British troops*
[2] *no one will question you, as you have not been in people's minds for so long, and are now shaggy and long-haired*
[3] *join the army*
[4] *what a shameful thing it is*

Guiderius declares, respectfully, that he will go to war with or without his father's permission. Belarius, persuaded by the two boys' fearlessness and determination, decides to join them:

Guiderius: By heavens, I'll go.
If you will bless me, sir, and give me leave,
I'll take the better care; but if you will not,
The hazard therefore due fall on me by
The hands of Romans.[1]
Arviragus: So say I, amen.
Belarius: No reason I, since of your lives you set
So slight a valuation, should reserve
My cracked[2] one to more care. Have with you,[3] boys.

[1] *I will accept that, as a result of my disobedience, I must face the perils of confronting the Romans*
[2] *impaired, ageing*
[3] *Come along; I'll go with you*

In Shakespeare's time, play scripts were generally the property of the theatre company for which they were written. They were a valuable asset – at least in the short term – and companies were generally unwilling to publish them, particularly while a play was still popular and attracting audiences. Half of Shakespeare's plays, for example, were not published during his lifetime.

While Shakespeare was undoubtedly involved in the publication of his sonnets and other poems, he seems to have shown little interest in the fate of his works for the stage. Plays were regarded as transient, short-lived creations rather than serious literature; and when Shakespeare's contemporary, the playwright Ben Jonson, published a complete edition of his own plays in 1616, he was widely ridiculed.

However, even though the publication of *The Workes of Benjamin Jonson* may have aroused a hostile reaction in the literary world, it set an important precedent. Five years after Shakespeare's death, John Heminges and Henry Condell, two of his fellow actors, set about the task of creating a complete edition of Shakespeare's plays, including introductory material and an engraving of the author. The resulting book, now known as the 'First Folio', was published in 1623. This collected edition contained many plays – including *Macbeth*, *Julius Caesar*, *Twelfth Night* and *Cymbeline* – which had never been printed before, and which would otherwise have been lost for ever.

Atonement

Pisanio, never doubting Imogen's integrity, is convinced that Posthumus was tricked into believing that she was unfaithful. Pisanio has no intention of carrying out Posthumus' command to kill Imogen; however, in order to keep his master's trust, he has decided to claim that he has done so. He has even, in response to Posthumus' demand for proof, sent him a bloodstained item of her clothing.

Posthumus is now back in Britain. He has been enlisted in the Roman invasion force, along with Iachimo and other Roman aristocrats. He is carrying Imogen's bloodied garment as he wanders, alone, outside the Roman camp.

Since receiving news of Imogen's death, Posthumus has had a profound change of heart. He bitterly regrets his extreme response to his wife's infidelity: her fault was trivial, and in no way warranted the terrible punishment he ordered. He wishes that Pisanio had not obeyed him so readily, or that the gods had struck him down before he sent the fateful letter demanding Imogen's death:

Posthumus: O Pisanio,
Every good servant does not[1] all commands;
No bond but[2] to do just ones. Gods, if you
Should have ta'en vengeance on my faults, I never
Had lived to put on this;[3] so had you saved
The noble Imogen to repent,[4] and struck
Me, wretch, more worth[5] your vengeance.

[1] *does not carry out*
[2] *your only obligation is*
[3] *if you had punished me for my bad intentions, I would have died before I could order Imogen's death*
[4] *as a result, her life would have been spared, and she would have had the chance to repent*
[5] *worthy of, deserving*

The gods may appear to be cruel and unpredictable, Posthumus reflects; but there must be a purpose behind their actions, and mortals can only resign themselves obediently to their wills.

Although Posthumus has supposedly come to Britain in support of the Roman invasion, he has no intention of harming his homeland. He has already, to his shame, caused the death of the king's only child, heiress to the throne:

Posthumus: I am brought hither
Among th'Italian gentry, and to fight
Against my lady's kingdom. 'Tis enough
That, Britain, I have killed thy mistress.[1] Peace,
I'll give no wound to thee.

[1] *princess, future queen*

Posthumus is wearing the fashionable clothes of an Italian nobleman; now, however, he hurriedly changes, taking on the guise of a British peasant. As a solitary, unknown individual in these ragged clothes he will fight to the death, he vows, for Imogen's sake:

Posthumus: So[1] I'll fight
Against the part[2] I come with; so I'll die
For thee, O Imogen, even for whom my life
Is every breath a death;[3] and thus unknown,
Pitied nor hated,[4] to the face of peril
Myself I'll dedicate.

[1] *in these clothes*
[2] *side; the Romans*
[3] *although I already die of remorse for your death with every breath I take*
[4] *anonymous, neither pitied nor hated*

Posthumus recalls that his father, Leonatus, had been a famous warrior in earlier wars against Rome. Calling on his ancestors to give him strength and courage, he sets off to join the British ranks.

A humiliating loss

The battle is raging. Amidst the noise, confusion and bloodshed, it is impossible to tell who has the upper hand as the opposing armies of Rome and Britain alternately surge forward and fall back.

Separated for a moment from the Roman ranks, Iachimo suddenly finds himself confronted by a shabbily dressed British peasant. To his disbelief and shame, Iachimo is left defeated and disarmed by the stranger. Unaware that he has just encountered Posthumus, he believes that he is paying the price for his false claim to have seduced Imogen:

Iachimo: The heaviness and guilt within my bosom
Takes off my manhood.[1] I have belied[2] a lady,
The princess of this country, and the air on't
Revengingly enfeebles me[3] …

[1] *has robbed me of my courage*
[2] *slandered, lied about*
[3] *the country's air, in revenge, has made me weak*

Iachimo realises, in despair, that the honours and titles he has received over the years are meaningless, even ridiculous, if he cannot defend himself against an untrained country dweller.

Turning the tide

Elsewhere on the battlefield, the Romans are starting to gain the advantage. At a crucial moment, as the British lines weaken, Cymbeline himself is captured. Defeat seems inevitable, and large numbers of Britons take flight along a nearby narrow lane.

A rallying cry is suddenly heard above the tumult of battle. Belarius and the two brothers have taken control of the entrance to the lane, and are spurring on their fellow Britons. If they stand their ground, they can defeat the Romans:

Belarius: Stand, stand! We have th'advantage of the ground,
The lane is guarded. Nothing routs us but
The villainy of our fears.[1]
Guiderius and Arviragus: Stand, stand and fight!

[1] *it is only our oppressive fear that makes us retreat*

Posthumus now joins Belarius and his boys, and together they succeed in rescuing Cymbeline. As the British counter-attack intensifies, there is mounting confusion and chaos among the Roman troops. The Roman leader, Caius Lucius, tells his young servant Fidele to escape to safety. There is tumultuous violence all around them:

Lucius: Away, boy, from the troops, and save thyself,
For friends kill friends, and the disorder's such
As war were hoodwinked.[1]

[1] *as if war itself were blindfolded and indiscriminate*

Lucius is pessimistic about his army's prospects: if they cannot obtain reinforcements to meet the reinvigorated British threat, they will soon be in serious trouble.

Why did Shakespeare choose the Welsh port of Milford Haven as such a crucial location in *Cymbeline*? The port is over two hundred miles from London, and may seem an odd choice as the landing place for an invading Roman army, as opposed to the Channel coast.

However, Milford Haven would have held a particular significance for an audience of Shakespeare's time. The arrival of Posthumus, who helps to save King Cymbeline, might remind them of the arrival of another important figure at the same harbour. The future King Henry VII, who defeated Richard III at Bosworth, bringing the decades-long Wars of the Roses to an end, had also landed here:

"It was the port at which Henry Tudor landed in 1485 to establish the Tudor dynasty, of which Elizabeth I was the last representative, and to which James I was keen to present himself as the natural successor, genetically (both his parents were direct descendants of Henry VII) and symbolically, inheriting Henry's role as unifier and peacemaker."

Roger Warren, Introduction to the Oxford Shakespeare edition of *Cymbeline*, 1998

A wish fulfilled

V, iii

The Roman invasion has been successfully driven back. Posthumus is describing the action to a nobleman who was among those who had fled at the start of the battle. He tells him how the Britons, their king captured, had been retreating desperately along a narrow pass, pursued by a bloodthirsty mob of Romans; there were so many dead and dying among the British that the lane was becoming impassable.

The situation changed suddenly, Posthumus reports, when a white-bearded countryman and two young men, hardly more than boys, had roused the retreating Britons, inspiring them to turn and face their attackers. The Romans were quickly driven back along the same narrow path, and were slaughtered in droves as they fled.

Posthumus becomes angry as the nobleman, who had not had the courage to take part in the action, casually expresses his surprise and admiration:

Lord: This was strange chance:[1]
A narrow lane, an old man, and two boys.
Posthumus: Nay, do not wonder[2] at it. You are made
Rather to wonder at the things you hear
Than to work any.[3]

[1] *a lucky, unexpected turn of events*
[2] *be amazed*
[3] *your role seems to be to marvel at heroic acts rather than take part in them yourself*

Perhaps the man should turn the episode into a light-hearted poem, Posthumus suggests sarcastically:

Posthumus: Will you rhyme upon't,
And vent it for a mock'ry?[1] Here is one:
'Two boys, an old man twice a boy,[2] a lane,
Preserved the Britons, was the Romans' bane.'[3]

[1] *recite it for public amusement*
[2] *in his second childhood; feeble and unsteady*
[3] *ruin, downfall*

The nobleman makes a hasty exit. Posthumus is scornful of the man's earlier flight from the conflict, but realises that many like him died despite their attempts to escape. Ironically, Posthumus himself, in the thick of the fighting, was unharmed despite the carnage all around him. Death is a strange creature, he reflects, and despite its ugliness is often found lurking in seemingly pleasant circumstances:

Posthumus: I, in mine own woe charmed,[1]
Could not find death where I did hear him groan,
Nor feel him where he struck.[2] Being an ugly monster,
'Tis strange he hides him in fresh cups, soft beds,
Sweet words[3] …

[1] *protected by my own misery, as if by a magic spell*
[2] *even when groaning and dying people were nearby*
[3] *refreshing drinks, comfortable beds, and flattering words*

Although he has remained safe throughout the battle, Posthumus is now ready to die. He has played his part in saving the nation of which his beloved Imogen was princess, and has no further reason to live.

There is one certain way to achieve his aim: he now discards his coarse, homespun garments and puts on instead the fine Italian clothes he was wearing earlier. These clearly mark him out as a Roman, and it will not be long before he is arrested by British troops. They will be in a vengeful frame of mind after the ferocious fighting that has just taken place.

A group of British soldiers now approaches, as Posthumus had hoped. They are discussing their victory over the Romans and the capture of Caius Lucius, the Roman leader. The identities of the four men who played such a decisive role in defeating the invaders – the white-bearded old man, his two young sons, and the peasant in ragged clothes – are still unknown.

There is a rumour that divine intervention was at work:

1st Captain: Great Jupiter be praised, Lucius is taken.
'Tis thought the old man and his sons were angels.
2nd Captain: There was a fourth man, in a silly habit,[1]
That gave th' affront[2] with them.
1st Captain: So 'tis reported,
But none of 'em can be found.

[1] *rustic clothes*
[2] *took part in the attack*

The soldiers suddenly notice Posthumus. They do not recognise him as the valiant Briton they have just mentioned; instead they take him, in his Italian clothes, for a member of the Roman army. When challenged, he responds defiantly that he would have led the Roman invaders to victory if he had been given the support he needed.

The soldiers, infuriated, seize Posthumus forcibly. Vowing that he will not live to return to Italy, they drag him away to be presented to the king.

Submission V, iv

In celebration of the British victory, Cymbeline and his followers are marching triumphantly across the battlefield. When the disguised Posthumus is brought before him, the king orders a jailer to take charge of their Roman captive. Posthumus is then unceremoniously shackled and left out in the open field, in chains, on his own.

Posthumus remains calm and uncomplaining; neither captivity nor death now holds any fear for him. It is his sense of guilt over Imogen's death that troubles him, not his own fate. The only way he can make amends, and prepare for his execution, is through deep, heartfelt repentance:

Posthumus: Most welcome, bondage, for thou art a way,
I think, to liberty.[1]
… My conscience, thou art fettered[2]
More than my shanks[3] and wrists. You good gods, give me
The penitent instrument to pick that bolt,[4]
Then free for ever.

[1] *you will lead to the final release of death*
[2] *chained, imprisoned*
[3] *legs*
[4] *repentance strong enough to unlock the guilt that binds me*

Posthumus asks the gods to accept the offer of his life as recompense for Imogen's death. It is a poor bargain, he accepts, but it is all he has to offer:

Posthumus: For Imogen's dear[1] life, take mine, and though
'Tis not so dear, yet 'tis a life; you coined[2] it.
… and so, great powers,
If you will make this audit,[3] take this life,
And cancel these cold bonds.[4]

[1] *beloved; valuable*
[2] *created, formed*
[3] *settle my account, discharge my debt*
[4] *release me from my worldly obligations*

Calling out to Imogen, Posthumus finally lies down on the cold, hard ground and falls asleep.

> *"The idea of death, or grief, as a transformative force is a feature of all of Shakespeare's late plays and it is, for me, the central idea of* Cymbeline. *By experiencing loss and grief all the characters learn the true value of relationships they previously took for granted. In the play, grief becomes a potential gateway to a form of spiritual rebirth."*
>
> Director Dominic Cooke on his 2003 production of *Cymbeline*

Down from the heavens

As Posthumus sleeps, the ghosts of his dead mother and father appear. His father, Sicilius Leonatus, a renowned warrior, is in the armour that he wore in his many battles with Rome. Posthumus' two brothers follow; they fought and died resisting Roman invaders, and their war wounds are clearly visible. To the sound of unearthly music, the four phantoms circle the sleeping figure on the ground.

Sicilius calls out to Jupiter, king of the gods. As Sicilius had died before his son was born, he was unable to protect him; Jupiter, as universal father, should have kept Posthumus safe from the misfortune that has afflicted him. Posthumus' mother too laments the fact that the gods did not come to her aid, but let her die in childbirth:

Sicilius: I died whilst in the womb he stayed,
  Attending nature's law,[1]
Whose father then – as men report
  Thou orphans' father art –
Thou shouldst have been, and shielded him
  From this earth-vexing smart.[2]
Mother: Lucina[3] lent me not her aid,
  But took me in my throes[4] …

[1] *waiting for nature to take its course*
[2] *suffering that torments mortals on earth*
[3] *goddess of childbirth*
[4] *took my life while I was in labour*

The four spirits are unanimous in their appeal to Jupiter: why has a man of such worth and promise, chosen by Britain's princess to be her husband, been allowed to fall into his present state of misery?

A noble mind, they complain, has been misled by a worthless villain:

Sicilius:	Why did you suffer[1] Iachimo,
	  Slight[2] thing of Italy,
	To taint his nobler heart[3] and brain
	  With needless jealousy,
	And to become the geck and scorn[4]
	  O'th' other's villainy?

[1] *allow*
[2] *insignificant, contemptible*
[3] *to infect Posthumus' superior temperament*
[4] *victim, laughing stock*

Posthumus' brothers point out that he has fought bravely in defence of his king and country, just as they did when Cymbeline's predecessor was on the throne. Sicilius begs Jupiter to help, and even threatens to appeal to the other gods. His sons add their voices to his plea:

Sicilius:	Peep through thy marble mansion,[1] help,
	  Or we poor ghosts will cry
	To th' shining synod of the rest
	  Against thy deity.[2]

Brothers:	Help, Jupiter, or we appeal, And from thy justice fly.[3]

[1] *the clouds which hide the heavens*
[2] *we will appeal against your judgement to the heavenly assembly of all the gods*
[3] *we will reject your authority*

The ghosts suddenly fall to their knees in amazement and terror. Flashes of lightning and deafening thunderclaps fill the air as the heavens open and Jupiter himself descends, seated on an eagle. It is clear that the king of the gods is displeased.

Jupiter angrily tells the ghostly visitors not to concern themselves with human affairs. It is his role, not theirs, to judge the actions of mortals and to intervene when he sees fit. There is a greater purpose, he reveals, behind Posthumus' suffering:

Jupiter: Whom best I love, I cross,[1] to make my gift,
The more delayed, delighted.[2] Be content.
Your low-laid son our godhead[3] will uplift;
His comforts thrive, his trials well are spent.[4]

[1] *I make their lives difficult*
[2] *so that the fulfilment of their desires, having been delayed, is appreciated all the more*
[3] *I, Jupiter*
[4] *I will ensure that his future is peaceful and happy, and that his suffering has been worth while*

Posthumus has always been a faithful follower of Jupiter, and the god intends to reward him accordingly:

Jupiter: Our Jovial star[1] reigned at his birth, and in
Our temple was he married. Rise, and fade.[2]
He shall be lord of Lady Imogen,
And happier much by his affliction made.

[1] *the planet Jupiter*
[2] *return to your home in the heavens*

Jupiter hands the ghosts a richly bound document, ordering them to lay it on Posthumus as he sleeps. With a final warning not to provoke his anger again, he commands his eagle to take him back up into the heavens. As Jupiter ascends, the ghosts are overwhelmed with gratitude and awe. They place the god's message on the sleeping figure on the ground: they then fade away, leaving Posthumus once more on his own.

In 1610, Shakespeare's contemporary Galileo published a book describing some observations he had made using a telescope, a recent invention which fascinated him, and which he had worked on intensively to improve and refine. Galileo's book, *Sidereus Nuncius* ('The Starry Messenger'), generated huge excitement; the illustrations showed, for the first time, many details of the heavens that were not visible to the naked eye. Although it was published in Venice, at least one copy of Galileo's book was brought to London at once, as was one of the new, improved telescopes.

One of Galileo's discoveries was that the planet Jupiter was orbited by four of its own moons. This was an extremely significant finding; it contradicted the age-old belief that all celestial bodies revolved around the Earth, which sat, eternal and unmoving, at the centre of the universe. This traditional view of the world was already being questioned, and *Sidereus Nuncius* reinforced the growing belief that the Earth was simply another planet, and revolved around the Sun.

Galileo's book brought him into conflict with the Catholic Church, which fiercely resisted any challenge to the established view: the Bible, they claimed, placed the Earth at the centre of the world, while the heavens revolved around it. Galileo tried to avoid controversy, but for many years he had an uneasy relationship with the church authorities. Eventually, suspected of heresy, he was tried by Catholic Inquisitors. He narrowly escaped being tortured, but his books were banned, and he spent the last ten years of his life under house arrest.

Shakespeare's stage direction for the four ghostly forms in Posthumus' dream is striking:

They circle Posthumus round as he lies sleeping.

By presenting the four circling figures, with the great Jupiter above them, was Shakespeare reminding his audience of Galileo's latest contribution to the world of science?

A puzzling message

On waking, Posthumus' first reaction is disappointment and frustration. He has never known his parents or his brothers, and to discover that their visit was nothing more than a dream has left him bereft. He quickly has second thoughts, however, and tells himself that he should be grateful for this brief glimpse of his family. He wonders whether magical forces are at work in the area; and his thought is confirmed when he discovers a mysterious, intricately bound document.

Posthumus hopes that the paper's contents are as significant as its appearance. On reading it, however, he remains unsure. The message is mysterious and unclear:

Whenas[1] a lion's whelp[2] shall, to himself unknown, without seeking find, and be embraced by a piece of tender air; and when from a stately cedar shall be lopped branches which, being dead many years, shall after revive, be jointed to the old stock, and freshly grow; then shall Posthumus end his miseries, Britain be fortunate and flourish in peace and plenty.

[1] *when*
[2] *cub*

Unable to decide whether the message is meaningful or not, Posthumus decides to keep it. After all, he reasons, his own life has already become strange and confusing:

Posthumus: 'Tis still a dream, or else such stuff as madmen
Tongue and brain not[1] …
Be what it is,
The action of my life is like it, which I'll keep,
If but for sympathy.[2]

[1] *say without thinking or understanding*
[2] *whatever this letter may be, it matches my life in its strangeness, and for no better reason than that I'll keep it*

Facing death

The jailer now returns. It is time for his Roman prisoner of war to face the hangman. Posthumus is cheerful and ready to meet his fate; the jailer, nevertheless, offers his sympathy and some homespun philosophy. Food and drink are on his mind, and he tries to console his prisoner with the thought that he will no longer face the consequences of overindulgence:

Jailer: A heavy reckoning[1] for you, sir. But the comfort is, you shall be called to no more payments, fear no more tavern bills, which are as often the sadness of parting as the procuring of mirth.[2]

[1] *a large bill; a sad outcome*
[2] *the size of which can make your visit painful rather than pleasant*

Posthumus is amused by the jailer's negative portrayal of a typical visit to a tavern:

Jailer: You come in faint for want of meat,[1] depart reeling with too much drink, sorry that you have paid too much, and sorry that you are paid too much,[2] purse and brain both empty …
Posthumus: I am merrier to die than thou art to live.

[1] *with hunger*
[2] *regretting that you have been punished so severely for the amount you have drunk*

The jailer finds it difficult to believe that the prisoner is willingly going to his death; surely he must be troubled by what may come afterwards? Again, Posthumus insists that he is perfectly ready for the next world:

Jailer: Indeed, sir, he that sleeps feels not the toothache, but a man that were to sleep your sleep, and a hangman to help him to bed, I think he would change places with his officer;[1] for look you, sir, you know not which way you shall go.[2]
Posthumus: Yes indeed do I, fellow.

[1] *the hangman*
[2] *where you will go after death; to heaven or hell*

A messenger now arrives, announcing that the prisoner is to be unchained and brought before the king. Posthumus is pleased, assuming that the time for his execution has come. The jailer, misunderstanding, thinks that the prisoner is expecting to be set free, and declares that he will not allow this to happen:

Messenger:	Knock off his manacles,[1] bring your prisoner to the king.
Posthumus:	Thou bring'st good news, I am called to be made free.[2]
Jailer:	I'll be hanged then.

[1] *remove his shackles, unchain him*
[2] *liberated through death; executed*

As he leads Posthumus away, the jailer reflects that his prisoner seems remarkably good-natured for a Roman; he has known others who are undoubtedly more deserving of execution and yet are desperate to avoid death. The supposed stoicism of Romans when facing execution is not always evident in reality, he observes. This does not surprise him; after all, he himself would do all he could to avoid the death penalty.

For a moment, the jailer wishes that the whole business of conflict and retribution could be brought to an end, even though it would put him out of work:

Jailer: … on my conscience, there are verier knaves desire to live, for all he be a Roman;[1] and there be some of them too that die against their wills; so should I, if I were one. I would we were all of one mind, and one mind good.[2] O, there were desolation of jailers and gallowses![3] I speak against my present profit[4] …

[1] *truly, despite the fact that he is a Roman, there are worse criminals than him who desire to live*
[2] *I wish we all lived in harmony, and had good intentions*
[3] *that would mean financial ruin for jailers and hangmen*
[4] *my own interests; my current source of income*

Treachery revealed

Now that the threat of invasion is over, Cymbeline has assembled his victorious troops and followers in the British camp near the battlefield. The king addresses the three men who saved his life and played such an important role in defeating the Roman invasion. He laments the fact that the soldier who fought alongside them – a peasant in threadbare clothes – is nowhere to be found:

Cymbeline: [*to Belarius, Guiderius and Arviragus*] Stand by my side, you whom the gods have made
Preservers of my throne. Woe is my heart
That the poor soldier that so richly fought,
Whose rags shamed gilded arms,[1] whose naked breast
Stepped before targes of proof,[2] cannot be found.

[1] *whose ragged clothes put those in glittering armour to shame*
[2] *who stepped into battle unprotected, ahead of those who carried shields of proven strength*

Cymbeline asks Belarius about himself. Afraid to reveal his true identity, as the courtier who abducted the king's sons many years ago, he gives a brief, cautious answer:

Cymbeline: 'Tis now the time
To ask of whence you are. Report it.
Belarius: Sir,
In Cambria[1] are we born, and gentlemen.
Further to boast were neither true nor modest,
Unless I add we are honest.

[1] *Wales*

Cymbeline draws his sword and knights Belarius, Guiderius and Arviragus: they are now honoured members of his court.

The mood of celebration suddenly changes when the royal physician Cornelius enters, along with a group of the queen's ladies-in-waiting. He has grim news: the queen is dead. She died in a state of mental torment, Cornelius reports, unable to hide her true feelings and intentions any longer. Her apparent devotion to Cymbeline was a pretence:

Cornelius: First, she confessed she never loved you, only
Affected greatness got by you[1] …

[1] *wanted the eminence and importance that she could achieve through marrying you*

Cymbeline is dismayed. There is worse to come, however:

Cornelius: Your daughter, whom she bore in hand[1] to love
With such integrity, she did confess
Was as a scorpion to her sight, whose life,
But that her flight prevented it, she had
Ta'en off by poison.[2]
Cymbeline: O most delicate[3] fiend!

[1] *pretended, claimed*
[2] *she intended to poison Imogen, and was only prevented by her sudden disappearance from court*
[3] *subtle, crafty*

The queen's ultimate ambition was for her son Cloten. Her plan was, first, to subject the king to a slow, lingering death:

Cornelius: She did confess she had
For you a mortal mineral[1] which, being took,
Should by the minute feed on life, and ling'ring,
By inches waste you.[2]

[1] *deadly powder, poison*
[2] *would eat away at you, gradually destroying your life*

The queen was confident that she could then persuade Cymbeline, as his life ebbed away, to designate Cloten as his successor:

Cornelius: In which time she purposed
By watching,[1] weeping, tendance,[2] kissing, to
O'ercome you with her show;[3] and in time,
When she had fitted you with her craft,[4] to work
Her son into th'adoption of the crown[5] ...

[1] *staying awake through the night and watching over you*
[2] *care, attention*
[3] *pretence*
[4] *cleverly moulded you into the right frame of mind*
[5] *contrive to have her son recognised as heir to the throne*

The queen's plan was thwarted by Cloten's sudden, unexplained disappearance, and she grew increasingly desperate at the lack of news of his whereabouts. Eventually she died in a frenzy of anger, frustration and regret.

The doctor's account is confirmed by the queen's maidservants. Cymbeline bitterly regrets his failure to see through his wife's deceit. It has had terrible consequences for one person above all, he realises sadly: his daughter, the princess Imogen.

> *"No fewer than four distinct worlds are evoked: classical Rome, Renaissance Italy, pagan Britain, and the abstracted countryside of pastoral romance, represented by Wales. The intricate reconciliation of these venues in the final scene requires such extraordinary ingenuity that it has inspired equal measures of praise and ridicule, as perhaps no other scene in Shakespeare has."*
>
> Charles Boyce, *Shakespeare A to Z*, 1990

A familiar face

A group of prisoners of war, guarded by British soldiers, is now led into the camp. The captives include the Roman leader, Caius Lucius, and his young servant Fidele; Iachimo is also with them, as is the unknown Italian soldier who impressed the jailer so greatly with his readiness for death.

Cymbeline addresses Caius Lucius first. On the last occasion they met, he remarks pointedly, Lucius – then the Roman ambassador – had demanded the payment of tribute, believing that Rome had the upper hand. The situation is very different now, the king announces gravely. Many British lives have been lost in the conflict, and it has been decided that all the captured Romans will be put to death.

Lucius accepts his fate, although Rome, he claims, would not behave in the same way. He hints, too, that the emperor may retaliate for such an action. His main concern, however, is for the life of his pageboy Fidele:

Lucius: This one thing only
I will entreat: my boy, a Briton born,
Let him be ransomed.[1] Never master had
A page so kind, so duteous, diligent,
So tender over his occasions,[2] true,
So feat,[3] so nurse-like …
… He hath done no Briton harm,
Though he have served a Roman.

[1] *let his life be spared, in return for payment*
[2] *sensitive to his master's requirements*
[3] *lively, graceful*

Cymbeline, feeling that he has seen the young servant somewhere before, willingly spares his life. The boy will be brought into the king's service at once:

Cymbeline: I have surely seen him;
His favour[1] is familiar to me. Boy,
Thou hast looked thyself into my grace,
And art mine own.[2]

[1] *face, appearance*
[2] *you have won my approval with your looks, and I welcome you as my own servant*

The king tells Fidele affectionately that he will grant anything the young boy wants; he will even spare the life of one of the prisoners if that is the boy's wish. Lucius is delighted, confident that Fidele will ask for his master to be saved. He is bitterly disappointed when the boy's attention turns elsewhere:

Lucius: I do not bid thee beg[1] my life, good lad,
And yet I know thou wilt.
Imogen: No, no, alack,[2]
There's other work at hand. I see a thing
Bitter to me as death. Your life, good master,
Must shuffle for[3] itself.

[1] *plead for*
[2] *unfortunately*
[3] *look out for, take care of*

Fidele's gaze is fixed on another of the Roman prisoners. Cymbeline is curious, wondering whether the man is a relative. Fidele replies that he is not, and asks to speak to the king in private.

Belarius and the two youths, meanwhile, are looking on in amazement. They are convinced that the boy speaking to the king is the very same boy who mysteriously appeared in their cave not long ago. Equally mysteriously, he had died suddenly, and Guiderius and Arviragus had laid his body on the ground, lovingly and dutifully, next to their mother's grave:

Belarius: Is not this boy revived from death?
Arviragus: One sand another
Not more resembles that sweet rosy lad
Who died and was Fidele.[1] What think you?
Guiderius: The same dead thing alive.[2]

[1] *one grain of sand does not resemble another more closely than this boy resembles Fidele*
[2] *the creature that we saw dead is now alive*

On further consideration, Belarius becomes more hesitant and uncertain. Still unwilling to reveal his identity or to invite further questioning, he tries to persuade the brothers that this may be a different Fidele.

Among the assembled Britons is Pisanio, servant to both Posthumus and Imogen. He too recognises the young pageboy, but unlike Belarius he is aware of Fidele's true identity beneath the disguise; it was Pisanio, in fact, who suggested that Imogen should disguise herself as a boy. Delighted that she is still alive and well, he nevertheless decides not to intervene for the time being:

Pisanio: [*aside*] It is my mistress.
Since she is living, let the time run on[1]
To good or bad.

[1] *let events take their course*

A confession

Fidele and his new master Cymbeline now return. Granted one wish, Fidele has not chosen to save the lives of any of the Roman captives. Instead, he wants to question one man in particular. That man is Iachimo; accordingly, the king orders him to come forward and answer his servant's question truthfully, on pain of torture. It emerges that Imogen has noticed a familiar diamond ring on Iachimo's finger. It is the ring that she gave Posthumus as he left Britain, banished by the king, and she is determined to know how it came into the Italian's possession:

Cymbeline: [*to Iachimo*] Sir, step you forth.
Give answer to this boy, and do it freely,
Or by our greatness and the grace of it,
Which is our honour, bitter torture shall
Winnow[1] the truth from falsehood. [*to Imogen*] On, speak to him.

Imogen: My boon[2] is that this gentleman may render[3]
Of whom he had this ring.

[1] *separate, extract*
[2] *request*
[3] *declare, reveal*

Posthumus, who has been observing events from the background, is startled; why, he wonders, is the pageboy interested in the ring that Iachimo won from him in their wager? He listens intently as Iachimo, now filled with shame and regret, describes how the ring came to be his.

Finally telling the truth about his appalling deception comes as a welcome relief, Iachimo tells the king. He first expresses his admiration for Posthumus, the man he so cruelly tricked:

Iachimo: I am glad to be constrained to utter that
Which torments me to conceal. By villainy
I got this ring. 'Twas Leonatus'[1] jewel,
Whom thou didst banish, and – which more may grieve thee,
As it doth me – a nobler sir ne'er lived
'Twixt sky and ground.

[1] *Posthumus'*

Posthumus was not Iachimo's only victim; Imogen too was callously exploited. Overcome with remorse, Iachimo can barely speak about her. Cymbeline, desperate for news of his missing daughter, urges him to continue even though he deserves to be executed on the spot:

Iachimo: That paragon, thy daughter,
For whom my heart drops blood,[1] and my false spirits
Quail to remember – give me leave, I faint.
Cymbeline: My daughter? What of her? Renew thy strength.
I had rather thou shouldst live while nature will[2]
Than die ere I hear more.

[1] *loses blood, bleeds*
[2] *for the remainder of your natural life*

Iachimo's confession now comes pouring out in a confused, tormented outburst. He can hardly contain his anguish and regret as he remembers the arrival of the British stranger at Philario's house:

Iachimo: Upon a time – unhappy was the clock
That struck the hour; it was in Rome – accursed
The mansion where; 'twas at a feast – O would[1]
Our viands[2] had been poisoned …

[1] *I wish, if only*
[2] *food*

The conversation had been light-hearted at first, reports Iachimo, as the men boasted about the merits of the women of their respective countries. Posthumus had praised his wife Imogen while, with typical graciousness, he refused to criticise the women of any other country.

Iachimo, resentful and jealous, had then made the fateful wager:

Iachimó: … I, wretch,
Made scruple of[1] his praise and wagered with him
Pieces of gold 'gainst this[2] which then he wore
Upon his honoured finger, to attain
In suit the place of's bed[3] and win this ring
By hers and mine adultery.

[1] *questioned, disputed*
[2] *this diamond ring*
[3] *to gain, by successfully pursuing Imogen, Posthumus' place in her bed*

Iachimo describes his visit to Britain, and how he deviously obtained details of Imogen's bedchamber. He even succeeded in discovering intimate marks on her body; and, in a final act of deception, he stole her bracelet, the token of love and loyalty that her husband had given her as he left his homeland.

Posthumus, hearing this revelation, is devastated. He is already suffering unbearable guilt at the fact that he brought about Imogen's death; and his pain is now made even worse on learning that she was innocent of any wrongdoing. Furious with Iachimo for his trickery, and with himself for falling victim to it, he rushes forward to denounce the Italian:

Iachimo: … my practice so prevailed[1]
That I returned with simular[2] proof enough
To make the noble Leonatus mad
By wounding his belief in her renown …
… he could not
But think her bond of chastity quite cracked,
I having ta'en the forfeit.[3] Whereupon –
Methinks I see him now –
Posthumus: Ay, so thou dost,
Italian fiend! Ay me, most credulous fool,
Egregious murderer …

[1] *my cunning strategy was so successful*
[2] *simulated, false*
[3] *it was inevitable that he would think she had been disloyal, and that I had seduced her*

Full of rage and self-loathing, Posthumus confesses to the king that he is responsible for Imogen's death. He is more resolved than ever to die for his terrible offence and, calling out Imogen's name, submits himself for execution.

Imogen herself, still disguised as the pageboy Fidele, now comes forward. It is time, she has decided, to reveal her true identity and comfort her grieving husband. Posthumus, however, is furious that an unknown servant is trying to intrude on his misery, and he lashes out violently:

Posthumus: My queen, my life, my wife. O Imogen,
Imogen, Imogen!
Imogen: Peace, my lord. Hear, hear –
Posthumus: Shall's have a play of this? [1] Thou scornful page,
There lie thy part.[2] [*he strikes her down*]

[1] *must we turn this into a spectacle?*
[2] *play your part by lying on the ground*

> *Shall's have a play of this?*
>
> *"A play which positively flaunts its own improbabilities,* Cymbeline *draws attention to itself as a fictional construct. Coincidence, implausibility, and theatrical cliché are stressed throughout. It seems to have been important to Shakespeare that his audience, here, should never lose sight of the wires that make the puppets move."*
>
> Anne Barton, Programme notes for the RSC production of *Cymbeline*, 1974

Reunited

Pisanio is horrified to see Posthumus unwittingly strike his wife. As he leans over the unconscious Fidele and calls out for help, the mention of Imogen's name sends both Cymbeline and Posthumus into a whirl of confusion:

Pisanio: O gentlemen, help!
Mine and your mistress! O my lord Posthumus,
You ne'er killed Imogen till now.[1] Help, help!
[*to Imogen*] Mine honoured lady.
Cymbeline: Does the world go round?[2]
Posthumus: How comes these staggers[3] on me?

[1] *unknown to you, Imogen was alive, but you may have killed her now*
[2] *has the world gone mad?*
[3] *dizziness, bewilderment*

As Imogen recovers consciousness, Cymbeline can hardly contain his emotions at the possibility that this may indeed be his missing daughter:

Pisanio: Wake, my mistress.
Cymbeline: If this be so, the gods do mean to strike me
To death with mortal[1] joy.

[1] *overwhelming, unbearable*

Imogen soon revives, but her response as she sees Pisanio's concerned face hovering over her is far from pleased. When she last saw Pisanio, near Milford Haven, he had tried to kill her with his supposed remedy:

Pisanio: How fares my mistress?
Imogen: O, get thee from my sight!
Thou gav'st me poison. Dangerous fellow, hence![1]

[1] *get away*

Pisanio defends himself passionately. The medicine was a valuable restorative, he claims, given to him by the queen. At this point Cornelius, the physician, cuts in. The queen had an obsession with poisons, he tells Cymbeline, and often asked him to prepare deadly compounds. She always claimed that they would only be used on small animals:

Cornelius: The queen, sir, very oft importuned me
To temper[1] poisons for her, still pretending
The satisfaction of her knowledge only[2]
In killing creatures vile, as[3] cats and dogs
Of no esteem.

[1] *urged me to concoct*
[2] *always alleging that she only wished to satisfy her curiosity*
[3] *such as*

Eventually Cornelius had agreed to supply the poison she wanted; however, suspecting her motives, he prepared instead a powerful sleeping potion. Whoever took it would appear to have died, but would later wake up reinvigorated. This is clearly what has happened to Imogen, he affirms; Pisanio is telling the truth. Hearing all this, Belarius realises that the visitor to their cave was indeed Imogen, disguised as Fidele. The body they laid so reverently on the ground had not, after all, been dead.

Imogen now turns to her husband Posthumus, and they embrace tenderly. He has rejected her once; it will never happen again. Even if he hurled her from the top of a cliff, says Imogen playfully, she would cling on to him. Posthumus too vows that their union will be lifelong:

Imogen: Why did you throw your wedded lady from you?
Think that you are upon a rock,[1] and now
Throw me again. [*she embraces him*]
Posthumus: Hang there like fruit,[2] my soul,[3]
Till the tree die.

[1] *at the top of a precipice*
[2] *like a vine clinging to a tree*
[3] *my love; Imogen*

Cymbeline was performed relatively rarely for two hundred years after Shakespeare's death; when staged, it was generally shortened and adapted to current tastes. However, the dreamlike quality of Shakespeare's original play appealed strongly to many Romantic and Victorian poets such as Keats, Swinburne and Tennyson:

"The strongest advocate for Cymbeline *in the nineteenth century was Tennyson, who was so fond of it that he asked for his copy on his deathbed. Fumbling with the volume ... he cracked the spine at his favourite passage,* 'Hang there like fruit, my soul, Till the tree die'*, and clasped the book until he died. Another copy was put in his hand for his burial at Westminster Abbey."*

Valerie Wayne, Introduction to the Arden Shakespeare edition of *Cymbeline*, 2017

The revelations continue

Cymbeline tearfully embraces his daughter. The queen is dead, he tells her gently, but the news causes her no grief. He mentions that the queen's son Cloten has mysteriously disappeared, and at this point Pisanio intervenes. He reveals that Cloten had forced him, on pain of death, to reveal Imogen's whereabouts. On learning that Imogen had gone to Milford Haven, Cloten had demanded some of Posthumus' clothes, and set off with evil intentions. Since then, Pisanio has had no news of him.

However, another member of the British camp knows exactly what happened to Cloten, and makes a dramatic declaration:

Pisanio: ... in a frenzy, in my master's garments,
Which he enforced from me,[1] away he posts[2]
With unchaste purpose, and with oath to violate
My lady's honour. What became of him,
I further know not.
Guiderius: Let me end the story:
I slew him there.

[1] *which he forced me to give him*
[2] *hurries, races*

The king is horrified. Even though he has just knighted the young man for the part he played in defeating the Romans, he has no choice; he has killed the queen's son, and must lose his life. Guiderius argues that Cloten deserved to die, but the king insists that the law must take its course:

Cymbeline: I am sorrow[1] for thee.
By thine own tongue thou art condemned, and must
Endure our law. Thou'rt dead.

[1] *I grieve*

The king's soldiers seize Guiderius. There is a further shock for the king, however, as another of the men he has just knighted, a white-bearded old warrior, steps forward and calls for Guiderius to be released:

Belarius: Stay,[1] sir king.
This man is better than the man he slew,
As well descended[2] as thyself…
Cymbeline: Why, old soldier,
Wilt thou undo the worth thou art unpaid for[3]
By tasting of our wrath?

[1] *stop, wait*
[2] *of equally noble descent*
[3] *squander the rewards that you have not yet been able to enjoy*

Belarius knows that he has put himself in mortal danger by challenging the king's authority. He warns Guiderius and Arviragus that, in telling the truth, he may forfeit his life even though it will help them; but the two boys vow to be loyal to their father whatever happens.

When Belarius reveals his true identity, the king's response is immediate and unequivocal. He is to be executed without delay:

Belarius: Thou hadst, great king, a subject who
Was called Belarius.
Cymbeline: What of him? He is
A banished traitor.
Belarius: He it is that hath
Assumed this age;[1] indeed a banished man,
I know not how a traitor.[2]
Cymbeline: Take him hence.
The whole world shall not save him.

[1] *he has reached my age; I am Belarius*
[2] *not a traitor, to the best of my knowledge*

Aware of the reaction that it will provoke, Belarius now hints at another astonishing revelation. As a traitor, he admits, all his property will be confiscated by the crown; but if money is under discussion, there is another consideration:

Belarius: Not too hot.[1]
First pay me for the nursing[2] of thy sons,
And let it be confiscate all so soon
As I have received it.[3]
Cymbeline: Nursing of my sons?

[1] *don't be too hasty*
[2] *raising, upbringing*
[3] *then you may immediately confiscate all my money*

Cymbeline, whose sons disappeared almost twenty years ago, is almost speechless. Belarius, kneeling before the king, recounts how he abducted the two boys with the help of their nurse Euriphile. He acted out of anger at his unjust banishment; despite his good name and honourable conduct, he explains, malicious courtiers had persuaded the king that he was a traitor.

It is time for the two brothers to take their rightful places at court, says Belarius: just as he is no longer the Welsh countryman Morgan, they are not Polydore and Cadwal any more, but the royal princes Guiderius and Arviragus.

Belarius still has the shawl in which the younger child was wrapped when he was first taken from court, and he offers to show it to Cymbeline as proof of his account. However, more immediate evidence is close at hand. Belarius reveals that, as Cymbeline recalls, the older brother has an unmistakable birthmark:

Cymbeline: Guiderius had
Upon his neck a mole, a sanguine[1] star:
It was a mark of wonder.[2]
Belarius: This is he,
Who hath upon him still that natural stamp.[3]
It was wise nature's end in the donation
To be his evidence now.[4]

[1] *blood-red*
[2] *wonderful, unique*
[3] *distinguishing mark*
[4] *it was nature's intention, in giving him this birthmark, that we should now be able to identify him*

Forgiveness

Cymbeline is overjoyed that all three of his children are back with him once more, safe and well. With the return of his older son Guiderius, Cymbeline remarks regretfully, Imogen is no longer heiress to the throne of Britain. Being reunited with her brothers is a far greater prize, she answers:

Cymbeline: O, what am I?
A mother to the birth of three? Ne'er mother
Rejoiced deliverance more.[1] Blest pray you be,
That after this strange starting from your orbs,
You may reign in them now.[2] O Imogen,
Thou hast lost by this a kingdom.
Imogen: No, my lord,
I have got[3] two worlds by't.

[1] *no mother ever rejoiced more at the delivery of her child*
[2] *after being unnaturally displaced from your rightful spheres, you can now resume your royal status*
[3] *gained*

Cymbeline has countless questions to ask his new-found children about the long, eventful journeys that have led them to this happy reunion; but first they must all give thanks and celebrate, in the traditional way, by burning sacrifices at the temple of Jupiter.

Swept along in the general mood of warmth and rejoicing, Cymbeline announces that even the Roman prisoners will be treated with clemency. It is a pity, he remarks, that the British peasant who fought so valiantly to save his life is not present.

Posthumus reveals that he was that poor, ragged individual. He then singles out Iachimo from the assembled prisoners and reminds him of their earlier encounter, when the Italian was disarmed:

Posthumus: I am, sir,
The soldier that did company these three
In poor beseeming[1] …
That I was he,
Speak,[2] Iachimo: I had you down and might
Have made you finish.[3]

[1] *fought alongside Belarius, Guiderius and Arviragus, dressed in rags*
[2] *you can confirm*
[3] *killed you, brought your life to an end*

Iachimo kneels. Painfully aware of the suffering he has caused, he is ready and willing to die. As his final act, he hands Posthumus the diamond ring that he deceitfully won in their wager, and the bracelet that he stole from Imogen as she slept.

Posthumus does not, however, take revenge on Iachimo. Cymbeline, moved by Posthumus' compassion, announces that all the Roman captives will be set free:

Posthumus: Kneel not to me.
The power that I have on you is to spare you,
The malice towards you to forgive you.[1] Live,
And deal with others better.
Cymbeline: Nobly doomed![2]
We'll learn our freeness[3] of a son-in-law:
Pardon's the word to all.

[1] *instead of using my power to kill you, I will spare you; and instead of displaying malice, I will forgive you*
[2] *pronounced, decreed*
[3] *generosity, benevolence*

... Pardon's the word to all.

The patron of the King's Men, Shakespeare's theatre company, was King James himself, a great lover of plays and shows of all kinds. The king prided himself on keeping the nation at peace, in particular bringing to an end the long, costly conflict with Spain.

King Cymbeline's reign coincided with two significant circumstances: the rule of the emperor Augustus, who established a long period of peace and stability in the Roman Empire; and the birth of Jesus Christ, the 'Prince of Peace'. As a character, Cymbeline is not without his flaws. However, in this final scene, is Shakespeare hinting at a parallel between the king on stage and his own royal benefactor?

"The reign of King Cymbeline spanned the time of universal peace – the Pax Romana *– during which Jesus Christ was born in Bethlehem; and the current king, James I, who liked to be known as* Jacobus Pacificus*, prided himself especially on his achievements as a peacemaker who had brought about the union of the British Isles."*

Stanley Wells, *Shakespeare: A Dramatic Life*, 1994

A new start

Caius Lucius and his soothsayer are among the released Roman prisoners. Posthumus now approaches them and describes the strange dream that he had while sleeping, in chains and condemned to death, on the battlefield. His ancestors had appeared to him, and eventually the great Jupiter himself seemed to descend from the heavens; stranger still, Posthumus reports, he found a short, beautifully bound manuscript lying on his chest when he awoke.

The soothsayer reads the message:

> *Whenas a lion's whelp shall, to himself unknown, without seeking find, and be embraced by a piece of tender air ...*

The lion's whelp, explains the soothsayer, refers to Posthumus; his family name, Leonatus, means 'born of a lion' in Latin. 'Tender air' is translated as '*mollis aer*' in Latin, similar to the term for a woman, '*mulier*'; this, then, refers to Imogen, who has just embraced Posthumus, although he did not at first recognise her in her disguise as Fidele.

The rest of the message concerns Cymbeline and his sons:

> *... and when from a stately cedar shall be lopped branches which, being dead many years, shall after revive, be jointed to the old stock, and freshly grow; then shall Posthumus end his miseries, Britain be fortunate and flourish in peace and plenty.*

The lopped branches, the soothsayer believes, are Guiderius and Arviragus, believed for many years to be dead but now reunited with their father. In short, Jupiter foresees that the reunion of Posthumus and Imogen, along with the homecoming of the king's two sons, will mark the beginning of an era of peace and prosperity for Britain.

Cymbeline resolves to play his part in achieving the harmony prophesied by Jupiter. Britain will live in peace with Rome, he announces; and even though the Roman invaders have been defeated, Britain will resume the payment of tribute to the empire, as agreed long ago. It was under the destructive influence of the queen and her son – both severely punished by the heavens – that the payments had ceased:

Cymbeline: Well,
My peace we will begin. And Caius Lucius,
Although the victor, we submit to Caesar,
And to the Roman Empire, promising
To pay our wonted[1] tribute, from the which
We were dissuaded by our wicked queen,
Whom heavens in justice both on her and hers
Have laid most heavy hand.[2]

[1] *customary, time-honoured*
[2] *have meted out harsh punishments both to her and to her son Cloten*

> *"... all the tangled strands of plot unravel in a brilliantly constructed series of revelations, and everyone receives their just reward. The villains die, Imogen and Posthumus are reunited, and King Cymbeline's abducted sons are restored to him. Indeed, while the play invokes famous tragedies, these invocations heighten the relief at what* doesn't *happen. The king errs in his marriage and his treatment of Rome, but his kingdom survives; Imogen and Posthumus both mistakenly believe the other to be dead, but they do not kill themselves out of deluded grief; Cymbeline loses his sons but gets them back; the Romans are defeated but their lives are spared. Tragedy looms but never strikes."*
>
> SparkNotes Editors, Analysis of *Cymbeline*, 2005

The soothsayer recalls his own dream on the eve of the battle with the British defenders. He had seen an eagle, he remembers, flying west and disappearing in the dazzling sunlight. The significance of his vision is now clear. Rome and Britain are destined to be allies, not enemies:

Soothsayer: The fingers of the powers above do tune
The harmony of this peace.[1]
… the Roman eagle
From south to west on wing soaring aloft,
Lessened herself,[2] and in the beams o'th' sun
So vanished; which foreshowed our princely eagle,
Th'imperial Caesar, should again unite
His favour with the radiant Cymbeline,
Which shines here in the west.

[1] *in presiding over this peace, the gods are creating harmony as if they were tuning a musical instrument*
[2] *gradually faded into the distance*

It is time to leave the military camp and head for London, where they will assemble at the temple of Jupiter, king of the gods, honoured equally by Britons and Romans. There, with sacrifices to the heavens and joyous celebrations, a formal declaration of peace will be made. Marvelling at the speed with which conflict has been transformed into harmony, Cymbeline urges everyone, Britons and Romans alike, to join him:

Cymbeline: Set we forward.[1] Let
A Roman and a British ensign[2] wave
Friendly together. So through Lud's town march,
And in the temple of great Jupiter
Our peace we'll ratify, seal it with feasts.
Set on there![3] Never was a war did cease,
Ere bloody hands were washed,[4] with such a peace.

[1] *let us go forth*
[2] *flag, banner*
[3] *forward march!*
[4] *even before the blood of battle was washed from the soldiers' hands*

Acknowledgements

The following publications have proved invaluable as sources of factual information and critical insight:

- Anne Barton, Programme notes for the RSC production of *Cymbeline*, RSC Publications, 1974
- Jonathan Bate, *Soul of the Age*, Penguin, 2008
- Jonathan Bate and Will Sharpe, Introduction to the RSC edition of *Cymbeline*, Macmillan, 2011
- Harold Bloom, *Shakespeare: The Invention of the Human*, HarperCollins, 1998
- Charles Boyce, *Shakespeare A to Z*, Roundtable Press, 1990
- Barry Cunliffe, Programme notes for the RSC production of *Cymbeline*, RSC Publications, 1989
- Nicholas Fogg, *Hidden Shakespeare*, Amberley, 2013
- Jennifer Forsyth, Introduction to *Cymbeline* in *Internet Shakespeare Editions*, University of Victoria, internetshakespeare.uvic.ca/doc/Cym_GenIntro/complete/index.htm, 2020
- Levi Fox, *The Shakespeare Handbook*, Bodley Head, 1987
- Harold C. Goddard, *The Meaning of Shakespeare*, University of Chicago Press, 1951
- Harley Granville-Barker, *Prefaces to Shakespeare*, Batsford, 1930
- Laurie Maguire and Emma Smith, *30 Great Myths about Shakespeare*, Wiley-Blackwell, 2013
- Will Sharpe and Kevin Wright, *The Director's Cut*, RSC Shakespeare edition of *Cymbeline*, Macmillan, 2011

- SparkNotes Editors, Analysis of *Cymbeline*, sparknotes.com/shakespeare/cymbeline/section8, SparkNotes LLC, 2005

- John Wain, *The Living World of Shakespeare*, Penguin, 1964

- Roger Warren, Introduction to the Oxford Shakespeare edition of *Cymbeline*, Oxford University Press, 1998

- Valerie Wayne, Introduction to the Arden Shakespeare edition of *Cymbeline*, Bloomsbury, 2017

- Stanley Wells, *Shakespeare: A Dramatic Life*, Sinclair-Stevenson, 1994

- Michael Wood, *In Search of Shakespeare*, BBC Books, 2005

Guides currently available in the *Shakespeare Handbooks* series are:

- ❑ **Antony & Cleopatra** (ISBN 978 1 899747 02 3)
- ❑ **As You Like It** (ISBN 978 1 899747 00 9)
- ❑ **The Comedy of Errors** (ISBN 978 1 899747 16 0)
- ❑ **Cymbeline** (ISBN 978 1 899747 20 7)
- ❑ **Hamlet** (ISBN 978 1 899747 07 8)
- ❑ **Henry IV, Part 1** (ISBN 978 1 899747 05 4)
- ❑ **Julius Caesar** (ISBN 978 1 899747 11 5)
- ❑ **King Lear** (ISBN 978 1 899747 03 0)
- ❑ **Macbeth** (ISBN 978 1 899747 04 7)
- ❑ **Measure for Measure** (ISBN 978 1 899747 14 6)
- ❑ **The Merchant of Venice** (ISBN 978 1 899747 13 9)
- ❑ **The Merry Wives of Windsor** (ISBN 978 1 899747 18 4)
- ❑ **A Midsummer Night's Dream** (ISBN 978 1 899747 09 2)
- ❑ **Much Ado About Nothing** (ISBN 978 1 899747 17 7)
- ❑ **Othello** (ISBN 978 1 899747 12 2)
- ❑ **Richard II** (ISBN 978 1 899747 19 1)
- ❑ **Romeo & Juliet** (ISBN 978 1 899747 10 8)
- ❑ **The Tempest** (ISBN 978 1 899747 08 5)
- ❑ **Twelfth Night** (ISBN 978 1 899747 01 6)
- ❑ **The Winter's Tale** (ISBN 978 1 899747 15 3)

www.shakespeare-handbooks.com

Printed in Great Britain
by Amazon